The **Droid** Pock **et Guide**

Second **2nd ed.** ~~Edition~~

Jason D. **O'Grady**

Ginormous knowledge, pocket-sized

DISCARDS

D1291799

The Droid Pocket Guide, Second Edition

Jason D. O'Grady

Peachpit Press
1249 Eighth Street
Berkeley, CA 94710
510/524-2178
510/524-2221 (fax)

Find us on the Web at: www.peachpit.com
To report errors, please send a note to errata@peachpit.com.

Peachpit Press is a division of Pearson Education.

Copyright © 2011 by Jason D. O'Grady

Executive editor: Clifford Colby
Editor: Kathy Simpson
Production editor: Tracey Croom
Compositor: David Van Ness
Indexer: Valerie Haynes Perry
Cover design: Peachpit Press
Interior design: Peachpit Press

ISBN-13:   978-0-321-74742-6
ISBN-10:   0-321-74742-9

9 8 7 6 5 4 3 2 1

Printed and bound in the United States of America

For Ginger and Graham

About the Author

Gadget guru Jason O'Grady has been writing about tech since the mid-'90s. His early affinity for Apple computers led him to start O'Grady's PowerPage (www.powerpage.org) in 1995, and readers began flocking to the site for news and information on issues that no one else seemed to cover. Predating Google with his daily details and critical content, O'Grady is considered to be one of the fathers of blogging.

His 2006 victory in a major legal battle with Apple paved the way for independent journalists everywhere, assuring bloggers of the same protections under the First Amendment as employees of mainstream media companies.

O'Grady is the author of *The Garmin nüvi Pocket Guide, The Nexus One Pocket Guide,* and the *Google Phone Pocket Guide* (Peachpit Press), and *Corporations That Changed the World: Apple Inc.* (Greenwood Press), as well as a contributor to the eighth and ninth editions of the *Mac Bible* (Peachpit Press), and has contributed to numerous Mac publications over the years. He's currently blogging about Apple for ZDNet at The Apple Core (www.zdnet.com).

Acknowledgments

I want to extend a huge "thank you" to everyone who made this book a reality.

Thanks to the team at Peachpit Press: Cliff Colby, who stalked me on Twitter and offered to have my house cleaned because I was procrastination-cleaning instead of writing; my editor, Kathy Simpson, for keeping the touch, press, key, and button references under control; production editor Tracey Croom, compositor David Van Ness, indexer Valerie Haynes Perry; and Cory Borman for the amazing cover.

Thanks to Sheldon Jones at Verizon Wireless and Pam Boyd at Thomas/ Boyd Communications for loaning me the Droids I was looking for. Jason Kaplan helped me embroider my bio with adjectives that don't suck.

This book was written on a MacBook Pro 15-inch using Dropbox for online storage, backup, and sync. Microsoft Word remains the de facto word processor in publishing, so I used Word 11 for the Mac. Screen shots were mostly captured in DDMS (via the Android SDK and Eclipse) and edited in Adobe Photoshop CS5 (thank you, Automate > Batch!). Pesky screens were rooted and shot with Screenshot It, by Edward Kim.

My other creature comforts while writing were a 27-inch Apple LED display and a pair of M-Audio AV40 speakers. The soundtrack for this book consisted primarily of Thievery Corporation, because its super-chill loungy style is my favorite to listen to while writing. My fallback genre is dub reggae (Scientist, Augustus Pablo, Dubblestandart, and Lee "Scratch" Perry), which I rock on Pandora One with some Pretty Lights, Girl Talk, MGMT, and 80s thrown in for good measure.

Most of all, special thanks to my parents; my wife, Liz; and my kids, Ginger and Graham. They loved me, fed me, and entertained me along the way. I couldn't have done it without them.

Contents

Introduction

Welcome to the second edition of *The Droid Pocket Guide*. Boy, has a lot changed in a year! Take a gander at how much the Android world has changed since the first edition of this book came out in March 2010:

- Android's U.S. market share grew from 2 percent in 2009 to 24 percent in 2010.

- More than 70 Android phones were released, and Android device shipments grew from 6 million to 55 million.

- Android activations grew tenfold, from 30,000 to 300,000 per day.

- Android Market apps grew tenfold, from 20,000 to 200,000.

Droids continue to gain in popularity because they're powerful and packed with features. They're also popular because there's a Droid model for everyone's unique set of requirements.

As you start down the path to mastering your Droid, some background information will provide a good foundation of knowledge to build on.

History and Background

One of the most compelling features of the Droid is Google, started by Larry Page and Sergey Brin while they were students at Stanford University and incorporated in 1998. Google branched out into mobile search in 2000, delivering its fast, powerful search results to handheld devices such as smartphones.

 The name *Google* was derived from the word *googol*, which is 1 followed by 100 zeros, or 10^{100}.

Google can't make a smartphone by itself, however. It takes a trio of forces to get a mobile phone to market, with each playing a unique and crucial role. Rounding out the trio are Google's manufacturing partners (Motorola and HTC) and its U.S. carrier partner (Verizon Wireless). Let's take a look at the players:

- **Verizon Wireless.** Verizon Wireless operates the largest wireless voice and 3G network in the United States, serving 91 million voice and data customers. Headquartered in Basking Ridge, N.J., Verizon Wireless is a joint venture of Verizon Communications and Vodafone.

- **Motorola Mobility.** The Droid Bionic, Pro, 2, and X are manufactured by Motorola Mobility, the mobile arm of the multinational telecommunications company based in Schaumburg, Ill. Motorola's mobile-devices division is focusing on smartphones using Android and will continue creating new smartphones, such as the Droid, Bravo, Defy, and Flipside phones that it launched in 2010.

- **HTC Corp.** The Droid Incredible is manufactured by HTC Corp., a Taiwanese firm founded in 1997. In 2006, the company launched a line of phones under its own brand name, and in 2009, it shifted focus to making phones based on Google's Android operating system (OS). HTC is the world's No. 4 smartphone brand and one of the fastest-growing companies in mobile technology.

The Dawn of Android

In 2005, Google acquired a company called Android with the intention of creating a carrier- and manufacturer-independent mobile OS that would run on almost any type of hardware. The Google Android (**Figure I.1**) is the logo and mascot of the OS of the same name and has become synonymous with mobile devices. I'd pick the Google Android over the Linux penguin in a fight any day.

Figure I.1
The Google Android, the mascot and logo of the mobile operating system.

The world got its first chance to use the new Android OS on October 22, 2008, when T-Mobile released the G1 smartphone in the United States. The G1 is sometimes referred to as the Google Phone. (Did I mention that I wrote a *Pocket Guide* for it too?)

What is Android?

Android is an open-source operating system, meaning that it's free to use and modify under the Apache and General Public License (GPL) licenses, which makes it very appealing to developers. Everyone from mobile-phone carriers to handset manufacturers to individual developers can modify the OS to accommodate specific needs. No costly licensing fees or restrictions are associated with Android, as there are with other operating systems. Developers are embracing Android because of its open-source roots and are signing up in droves to create applications (referred to as *apps*) for the Android Market, which I cover in detail in Chapter 9.

note Droid is the hardware; Android is the software. I provide more details on both hardware and software in the next few chapters.

Google is investing a lot of time and money in the Android OS and is committed to making it a real competitor in the mobile-phone market. We're just starting to see the fruits of its labor. Android is now available on more than 100 devices (up from 20 a year ago) in many languages worldwide, and it leapfrogged Apple's iOS to become the No. 2 mobile OS for the three-month period ending in November 2010. (The top dog is industry heavyweight Research In Motion, manufacturer of the iconic BlackBerry.) Android has been adapted for use on tablets, e-readers, notebooks, smartphones, and even television sets, and it's so open that I wouldn't be surprised to see it running on my refrigerator door when I wake up one morning. (I hope that I won't be leaving the door open all night.)

Android code names

Android is a complex piece of software, but that doesn't mean its software engineers can't have any fun while they're working on it. Take, for example, the code names of the major Android releases:

- Android 1.5—Cupcake (April 2009)

- Android 1.6—Donut (September 2009)

- Android 2.0/2.1—Éclair (October 2009)

- Android 2.2—Froyo (May 2010)

- Android 2.3—Gingerbread (December 2010)

- Android 3.0—Honeycomb (January 2011)

They're all desserts, and their names are in alphabetical order. At press time, it's confirmed that Ice Cream Sandwich will be the next major release of Android, available in June or July 2011. Google's engineers must have a sweet tooth or a playful sense of humor—or, as I suspect, both.

Name That Dessert

Android's alphabetical naming conventions leave many people wondering which ones will come after Ice Cream Sandwich. Here are some of my guesses:

- J—Jelly

- K—Kiwi (yes, fruit can be dessert)

- L—Licorice, Lemon Tart

- M—Marshmallow, Mousse, Meringue, Maple

- N—Nut, Nougat

- O—Orange Chiffon Cake

If the funny code names weren't enough, Google also has a tradition of announcing new versions of Android by erecting large dessert-shaped sculptures (**Figure I.2**) on the lawn in front of the Googleplex in Mountain View, California.

Figure I.2
Statues of the various Android code names adorn the lawn at the Googleplex.
COURTESY OF KARI MARIE

What To Expect

Finally, some housekeeping is order:

- This edition of *The Droid Pocket Guide* covers the Droid brand of mobile phones made by Motorola and HTC Corp., sold in the United States by Verizon Wireless. If you're using a Droid in another country or on another carrier, some screens and icons may look slightly different, but you should still be able to find your way around pretty easily with the help of this book.

 If you're using a Droid 1 (the original Droid) or Droid Eris, please check out *The Droid Pocket Guide, First Edition,* **which covers those devices.**

- This guide covers five Droid handsets on the market as of February 2011: the Droid Bionic, Pro, 2, and X (Motorola), and the Droid

Incredible (HTC). (See Chapter 1 for details.) I refer to all these hand-sets generically as *Droid* unless I want to differentiate a feature of a particular model.

■ Screen shots in this guide are mostly from the Droid X running Android version 2.2 (aka Froyo), but most of the content will remain relevant in Android 2.3 (Gingerbread) and later.

■ The Droid X runs a customized Android user interface that Motorola calls *Blur* or *MotoBlur*. If you're not using an HTC Droid (such as the Droid Incredible), some icons and screens will appear slightly different from those in this guide, but don't panic; the concepts are the same.

■ If your Droid is running a version of Android earlier than 2.2, you may not have some features in this guide. Check your version (touch Settings > About Phone > *version*), and upgrade your Droid's software to the latest version to take advantage of the newest features and bug fixes. You can upgrade on the Droid itself by navigating to Settings > About Phone > System Update.

■ Because of Android's open-source roots, any wireless carrier (or user, for that matter) can modify the look and feel of Android to suit its needs. For this reason, some screens, icons, and behaviors may be slightly different from what you find in this guide.

Welcome to Droid

It's time to take a look at the high-tech beast that is the Droid. The problem is that there isn't just one Droid but an army of Droids. In this chapter, I review the important specs and major features of seven models, from the original Droid to the rip-snortin' Droid Bionic.

Features

You have several good reasons to purchase a Droid, including the fact that its capabilities and features are always expanding. In fact, one of the biggest advantages of owning a smartphone—any smartphone—is that you can customize it infinitely by adding your own software. If you're a developer, you can create apps yourself; all the rest of us download them from the Android Market (see Chapter 9).

In this section, I take a look at core features that come with the Android operating system installed on the Droid.

Mobile phone

One of the primary reasons to buy a Droid is to get its phone, right? Most people would answer yes, but in reality, Droids do much more than just make phone calls. In fact, a whole generation growing up right now rarely (if ever) makes phone calls. Kids today communicate via Facebook, Twitter, Skype, and messaging services, using a phone only when they have to—like when their parents call.

A Droid is more akin to a computer than to a phone. Each year, mobile devices get smaller and faster at a seemingly exponential rate, and the Droid is a leader of the pack, offering a huge number of features.

I cover the phone in detail in Chapter 5.

Email

Another important reason to buy a smartphone is to keep up with your ever-growing pile of email. The Droid allows you to stay on top of your mail with ease.

The included Email app seamlessly syncs messages from most POP3 (Post Office Protocol Version 3) and IMAP (Internet Message Access

Protocol) services, and displays graphics and photos inline courtesy of its rich HTML viewer.

Droids also support corporate email servers running Microsoft Exchange—good news for business users. The Email app can find people in your company's global address list and will even autocomplete recipient names from the directory. Corporate IT departments will also appreciate the Droid's remote-wipe, data security, and encryption capabilities.

If you use Gmail exclusively, you're in luck: Android includes a dedicated Gmail application. Gmail for Android offers many of the same features as its desktop-based big brother, including search, stars and labels, archive, mute, move, and conversation view. Gmail offers two-way synchronization of email in real time (also known as *push*), so you'll get notified when you receive new emails, even if you're in another application. It even syncs draft emails, so you can begin writing a message on the Web and send it from the phone (and vice versa).

See Chapter 6 for more on email.

Messaging

Short Message Service (SMS) and Multimedia Messaging Service (MMS)—texting services, in mobile parlance—are extremely useful tools. Android's Messaging app provides both tools in one convenient location where you can read and reply to messages from your friends and colleagues. Received messages are threaded into a virtual conversation, making it easy to remember where you left off while bouncing among messages from different senders. The Android Messaging app also makes it easy to flag, delete, and move groups of messages.

In addition, the Messaging app allows you to add all your various email accounts and view them in a convenient universal inbox. Touching this inbox displays a convenient river of all of your email in reverse chrono-logical river. It sure beats having to check numerous inboxes if you have a lot of email accounts.

I cover messaging on the Droid in Chapter 6.

Browser

Android's integrated Browser app combines Google's legendary search capability with a mobile version of its desktop Web browser, Chrome. Google chose the open-source WebKit engine for its Android browser, which also powers Apple's Safari and Nokia's S60 browsers. It's a full HTML Web browser with the additional benefits of multitouch and voice search, so in some ways, it's actually better than a desktop browser.

Browser got a big performance boost in Android 2.2 (Froyo) with the addition of a just-in-time compiler and a speedy V8 JavaScript engine inherited from Chrome. And if that weren't enough, the Froyo browser includes Adobe Flash and a bunch of cool HTML 5 features that let you access device hardware—such as the accelerometer (for rotating the screen), the camera, and the microphone—from inside Web apps.

 Flash is a defining feature of the Android platform that isn't available on iOS devices.

The Browser app gained a dedicated shortcut key on the home screen in Android 2.2. Also, the app can display multiple pages concurrently, and its bookmark and history interface is similar to what you'd expect from your desktop Web browser.

Finally, to illustrate the fact that Google thought of everything, Browser includes *favicons:* the little graphics that appear before the URL and before the <title> tag in browser tabs.

See Chapter 6 for more on Browser.

Contacts

A smartphone isn't very smart if it doesn't have someone to call. Google has chosen an interesting method to sync contacts back and forth to the Droid: Google Contacts (www.google.com/contacts).

When you boot up your Droid for the first time, you'll be asked to log in to your Google account. After you log in, your contacts are synced automatically with the phone.

note If you're already a Gmail user, all your Gmail contacts will synchronize with your phone automatically. As you'd expect with a phone from Google, services from Google are baked into every aspect of the Android operating system.

The beauty of this system is that it's completely transparent and requires no user intervention whatsoever. You don't have to worry about USB cables, Bluetooth, or synchronization software; your contacts just sync in the background.

The downside is that if you're not a Google Contacts user, you'll have to import or enter your contacts to sync them to your phone. Fortunately, the process is Web-based (which definitely beats entering the contacts on the phone manually), and Google Contacts has excellent import tools.

The system supports importing contacts in CSV (comma-separated values) file format from Microsoft Outlook, Outlook Express, Yahoo, and Hotmail.

See Chapter 5 for more on Contacts.

Calendar

Just like contacts, Droid calendars sync with Google Calendar (www.google.com/calendar). Whatever information is in your Google Calendar gets synced with your phone automatically in real time, in the background.

gCalendar (as I like to call it) is loaded with features, including sharing, syncing with mobile phones and desktop software, reminders, invitations, and offline mode—not to mention that it's completely free.

As with Google Contacts, if you're already a Calendar user, you're all set up. If you're not, you have a little work to do. Luckily, Calendar can easily import event information in iCal or CSV (Outlook) format. To get your calendars into Google, first export them from whatever software you're using now; then follow the import steps on the Google Calendar Web site.

I discuss Calendar in Chapter 5.

Maps and Navigation

Google set the standard for Web-based mapping services with Google Maps and continues that tradition on the Droid. One of the Droid's best features is Google's free Navigation app, which provides free, turn-by-turn Global Positioning System (GPS) navigation with voice guidance for driving or walking directions.

Maps and Navigation—and all location-based software applications, for that matter—are better on mobile devices than they are on the desktop because they use your mobile phone's GPS chip to pinpoint your location. You don't have to enter your location information manually, because the Droid already knows where you are.

Things get even better when you add voice recognition to the mix. Instead of having to type the name of the supermarket, dry cleaner, or bank that you're looking for, you can just speak the name, and Android will convert it to text (with impressive accuracy) and perform the search for you.

What's more, Google Street View provides virtual street-level exploration from within the Maps and Navigation apps, courtesy of millions of pictures taken from a street-level perspective. The Droid's built-in magnetometer (digital compass) orients Street View according to your position and allows you to navigate 360 degrees simply by moving the phone around in your hand.

I cover Maps, Navigation, and the growing field of location-based apps in Chapter 7.

YouTube

Google acquired YouTube in 2006 for $1.65 billion, and the child of this beautiful union is a mobile YouTube app designed for the Droid's small screen and footprint. Although YouTube is great for watching videos of dogs skateboarding, it's also the default video player for most applications on the phone. YouTube has lots of business applications too, but I can't think of any right now.

YouTube for Android is loaded with features, including a catalog of millions of keyword-searchable videos that you can browse (most popular, most viewed, top rated, most recent, and most discussed) and view in high quality. When you've found a video that you like, you can view its details and then favorite it, share it, rate it, and comment on it directly within the app.

In addition to viewing videos, you can upload videos to the popular video sharing site from both the YouTube and Camera apps. Also, you can log in to your YouTube account from the Droid and access your favorites, your playlists, and your own uploaded videos.

See Chapter 8 for details on using YouTube on your Droid.

Search

Google is the undisputed king of search, so it's pretty natural to expect excellent search on your Droid. You won't be disappointed. In addition to letting you perform pedestrian tasks like searching the Web for images, blogs, news, books, and businesses, the Droid allows you to search with your voice.

Voice search on the Droid is a powerful new feature that makes searching more convenient and safer than ever—especially while you're driving. It's available in the Web browser (where you'd expect it) and via the Quick Search box, which is a search widget for Android. The Quick Search box searches not only the Web, but also the content of your phone. You can scan apps, contacts, browser bookmarks, YouTube videos, music, and stock quotes, all directly from the search widget.

Because the Droid is location-aware (thanks to GPS), searches are even more relevant, finding the landmarks, retail stores, and services that are closest to you first. Although all this tracking and location-based stuff may sound a little Orwellian, GPS can be extremely powerful when it's put to good use. Besides, you don't have anything to hide, do you?

The Droids You're Looking For

A whopping 74 Android phones have come to market since the first edition of this book was published in March 2010, including five new Droids. In this section, I highlight the major specifications of each of the Droid models, old and new.

Droid 1

Release date: November 6, 2009

Manufacturer: Motorola

CPU: 550 MHz Arm Cortex A8

Screen size: 3.7 inches

Resolution: 480 x 854 (FWVGA)

Video capture: 720 x 480 at 30 frames per second (fps)

Camera: 5 megapixel

Battery: 1400 mAh

Weight: 6 ounces

Keyboard: Horizontal QWERTY slider

Noteworthy features: Micro SDHC support, Google Maps Navigation

Droid Eris (aka HTC Hero)

Release date: November 6, 2009

Manufacturer: HTC

CPU: 528 MHz Qualcomm MSM7600A

Screen size: 3.2 inches

Resolution: 320 x 480 (HVGA)

Video capture: 352 x 288

Camera: 5 megapixel

Battery: 1300 mAh

Weight: 4.23 ounces

Keyboard: Touchscreen

Noteworthy features: Custom UI Scenes, trackball, social widgets

Droid Incredible

Release date: April 29, 2010

Manufacturer: HTC

CPU: 1 GHz Qualcomm Snapdragon

Screen size: 3.7 inches

Resolution: 480 x 800 (WVGA)

Video capture: 720p

Camera: 8 megapixel

Battery: 1300 mAh

Weight: 4.6 ounces

Keyboard: Touchscreen

Noteworthy features: Dual LED flash, optical mouse, tethering

Droid X

MOTOROLA MOBILITY, INC.

Release date: July 15, 2010

Manufacturer: Motorola

CPU: 1 GHz TI OMAP3630-1000

Screen size: 4.3 inches

Resolution: 480 x 854 (FWVGA)

Video capture: 720p

Camera: 8 megapixel

Battery: 1540 mAh

Weight: 5.5 ounces

Keyboard: Touchscreen

Noteworthy features: Large screen, HDMI out, 3G wireless hotspot

Droid 2

MOTOROLA MOBILITY, INC.

Release date: August 12, 2010

Manufacturer: Motorola

CPU: 1 GHz OMAP 3620

Screen size: 3.7 inches

Resolution: 480 x 854 (FWVGA)

Video capture: 720p

Camera: 5 megapixel

Battery: 1400 mAh

Weight: 6 ounces

Keyboard: Horizontal QWERTY slider

Noteworthy features: Improved keyboard, Flash Player 10.1, 3G mobile hotspot

Droid Pro

Release date: November 18, 2010

Manufacturer: Motorola

CPU: 1 GHz TI OMAP

Screen size: 3.1 inches

Resolution: 320 x 480 (HVGA)

Video capture: 720 x 480 at 30 fps

Camera: 5 megapixel

Battery: 1420 mAh

Weight: 4.7 ounces

Keyboard: Vertical QWERTY

Noteworthy features: Global capable, enterprise ready

Droid Bionic

Release date: Second quarter 2011

Manufacturer: Motorola

CPU: NVIDIA Tegra 2 AP20H Dual Core

Screen size: 4.3 inches

Resolution: 540 x 960 (qHD)

Video capture: 720p

Cameras: 8 megapixel rear, 0.3 megapixel front

Battery: 1930 mAh

Weight: 5.6 ounces

Keyboard: Touchscreen

Noteworthy features: First Droid with 4G, dual-core processor, front camera

Accessories

I'll presume that you've already taken the liberty of liberating your new Droid from its box and that you've activated it on your carrier's network. If you're like me, you probably unboxed your Droid, booted it up, and made your first call before you left the store.

These days, most smartphones ship with pretty much the same accessories in their boxes. The problem is that smartphones never include enough accessories, as manufacturers look for ways to reduce costs and increase their bottom lines. This means that you'll probably have to purchase—at minimum—a decent case and a car charger.

 Because of the differences among Droid models, I deal with accessories on a general level in this guide.

What's included

Inside your Droid package (assuming that you didn't shred it into a million pieces in rabid anticipation), you'll usually find the following:

- Droid handset
- Rechargeable battery
- Compact USB wall charger
- USB-to-Micro USB cable (for charging via USB)
- microSD card
- Quick-start guide

The microSD card is usually preinstalled in a Droid handset, but it can be difficult to find. To access it, you usually need to slide the rear panel off and remove the battery. On most Droids, swapping microSD cards involves a shutdown-and-reboot process that takes several minutes.

 The largest microSD card shipping as of February 2011 is a 32 GB card, which you can buy for about $80.

What's not included

Although all the basics that you need to get started with your Droid are included in the box, you should consider purchasing a few extras:

- **3.5mm stereo headphones with microphone.** Remarkably, most Droids don't include earbuds with mics, meaning that you'll have to procure them on your own. The included buds are almost always terrible, though, so you're probably better off buying your own anyway. Expect to spend between $10 and $100, and make sure that they include a microphone for making phone and VoIP calls, voice searching, and recording voice memos.

- **Car charger.** A car charger is a requirement these days. If you like to keep your Droid's power-hungry radios and screen lit up all the time (and who doesn't?), your battery will drain faster than you can say "I'll call you back." Grab one for between $5 and $15, and make sure that it has the proper Micro USB plug on the end.

tip **If you plan to use your Droid with the excellent Car Mount for Droid from Motorola ($30), make sure that you buy a car charger with a cable long enough to reach the dashboard or windshield where you plan to mount it.**

- **Extra battery.** A second battery can be a lifesaver (literally) at times. Although the included battery is decent, if you like to use a lot of GPS, Wi-Fi, and Bluetooth between charges, you should probably buck up for an extra battery. Original-equipment batteries cost about $35 online, and although aftermarket batteries cost significantly less, I don't recommend using them.

tip Check the charge of stored rechargeable batteries periodically. Dormant batteries lose approximately 10 percent of their charge per month.

- **A real case**. A case is the single best thing you can do to protect your investment in your Droid. No case is included in the package, however, so you're on your own for this one. You can find hundreds of mobile-phone cases on the market, and making a choice can be deeply personal. I'll leave you to your own devices to find one that suits your needs and personality.

- **Screen cover/film**. If you tend to be as rough on your gadgets as I am, it's a good idea to invest in a screen film. This clear film sticks onto the screen of the phone, protecting it from scratches from keys, coins, and anything else that may be in your purse or pocket. Prices range from $3 to $15, and it's money well spent.

Now that you've taken a peek at the Droid's best features and accessories, it's time to get started using your Droid in Chapter 2.

2

Getting Started with Droid

In this chapter, I get into the nuts and bolts of setting up your Droid, including activating the phone and getting set up with Google. If you've already activated your Droid and linked it to your Google account, don't fret. This information will come in handy if you ever have to set up your Droid again (which happens occasionally) or if you need to help a friend with his Droid. Knowledge is power, so read on.

Setting up Your Droid

On its maiden boot, your Droid steps you through several setup screens that are very important in the overall scheme of things. These screens help you set up your Google account, which will be the primary account on your device. When you enter your Google account information, the Droid uses that information to sync your email, contacts, and calendar events from the cloud to your phone.

 This section assumes that you're setting up your Droid on the Verizon Wireless network in the United States.

Start me up

To turn your Droid on for the first time, press and hold the Power button. You'll be greeted by the friendly Android robot (**Figure 2.1**). Simply touch that image to begin.

Figure 2.1

The Android robot laughs like the Pillsbury Doughboy when you do this.

Activate the phone

First, you'll be prompted to activate your phone (**Figure 2.2**). Touch the
Activate button, and a special call is made to Verizon Wireless programming. To program or activate your phone, press 1 at the voice prompt.

 You can listen to instructions on how to set up your voicemail while
you're waiting for your programming to complete.

Figure 2.2
*The process of
activating your
Droid.*

When programming is complete, an onscreen message tells you that your Droid has been programmed successfully. Then you'll see a reassuring *Phone is activated!* message (refer to the bottom-right image in Figure 2.2). Touch Next in that screen to get some helpful instructions on using your Droid (**Figure 2.3**). If you're using a Droid for the first time, touch Begin and take the time to step through the tutorials; they'll pay dividends in the future. If you're a Droid veteran or just impatient, you can skip the tutorials by touching the handy Skip button.

Figure 2.3

Although it's tempting to touch Skip, I encourage you to take the tutorial.

Setting up Your Google Account

After you activate your Droid and take the tutorial, you'll see the Set up Your Google Account screen, which prompts you to set up your Google account (**Figure 2.4**).

Figure 2.4
*Time to set up
your Google
account.*

This screen gives you three options, two of which I cover in the following sections.

 Optionally, you can skip this part by touching the Skip button, but I don't recommend it. You're going to need to enter your Google credentials eventually, so why not just do it now?

Signing in to an existing account

If you already have a Google account, touch the Sign In button. In the resulting screen (**Figure 2.5** on the next page), enter your Google user name (or your Gmail address) and password; then touch the Sign in button in the bottom-right corner. When you sign in, you're agreeing to Google's terms and privacy policies, which you're required to do.

 Any Google login will work here. If you've got a Gmail, Google Docs, or other Google password, you can use it to sign in. If you have more than one Google account, link your Droid to the account you use most.

Figure 2.5

Enter the user name and password associated with your Google account.

 Usually, a Gmail account works best because it already has your email contacts in it.

Creating an account

Having a Google account is a critical part of owning a Droid, because this account allows you to keep your contacts, calendars, and email in sync. If you don't already have a Google account—and really, you don't?—touch the Create button in the Set up Your Google Account screen (refer to Figure 2.4), and follow the onscreen steps to create one from scratch.

After you've promised your life away to Google, you're on your way to Google bliss! (Actually, it's not that exciting; I take it back.)

In the next screen (**Figure 2.6**), you're warned that it could take an entire *5 minutes* to set up your account. Time to shovel the driveway! Don't be alarmed, though; my account took about a minute to set up on the Verizon Wireless network where I live.

Figure 2.6
After you enter your Google credentials, your Droid contacts Google to set up your account.

Providing location information

While your Droid is being linked to your Google account, it will ask you for consent to provide your location information anonymously to Google (**Figure 2.7**).

Figure 2.7
You can share your location with Google or keep it private.

If you want to use location-based apps or anything that uses GPS (like Maps and Navigation), you should check both boxes. Although I find location-based apps to be extremely compelling, they may not be your cup of tea, so if you're leery of sharing your location data with Google (or if your name is George Orwell), you have my permission to leave these boxes unchecked. Not to worry, though—you can always change your preferences later by touching Settings > Location & Security.

note One of the wonders of sharing your location information with Google is that Google uses this data to display real-time traffic information on its maps. Crowdsourced traffic reports are possible thanks to the millions of Android users who share their location data with Google. There—I hope that I guilted you into turning this feature on.

Deciding whether to back up

Hang tight—you're almost there. In the next screen, Google asks whether you'd like your app settings and other data to be backed up to its servers in the cloud (**Figure 2.8**). I highly recommend that you check

Figure 2.8
Google provides free data backup services that you should take advantage of.

the box in this screen and accept backup, because backup makes it easier to restore your Droid if you lose, break, or upgrade it. Google is committed to protecting your privacy and uses encryption when transmitting backup data to and from its servers.

If you accept data backup during setup but get concerned about it later, you can disable the functionality on your Droid by touching Settings > Privacy > Back up My Data. When you disable backup, Google deletes all saved backup data. Although you can reenable backups later, Google won't restore any previously deleted data.

Linking and syncing

The next step—syncing your account information—is quick and painless. Initially, Droid downloads just your basic account info from Google, not the thousands of emails, contacts, and calendar events you may have stored in the cloud. After your account info is synced for the first time, your contacts, calendar events, and email download to your phone in the background (**Figure 2.9**).

Figure 2.9
Your Google account and Droid are linked now. Congrats!

Your Google Account is now linked to this phone.

Google applications are syncing data now.

When the "syncing" icon disappears from the status bar at the top of your screen, the download has finished.

About the status bar...
Whenever you receive a new message or other notification, an icon appears in the status bar.

Use your finger to drag down the status bar to open the Notifications panel, with details about all your current

Finish setup

When the syncing icon disappears from the status bar at the top of the screen (see "Knowing Your Notifications" in Chapter 3), the download is complete.

Exploring Your Droid

Now that your Droid is set up and accessing the Internet, it's time to put down this guide for a bit and have some fun. If you know how to use the Internet, you already know how to use the Droid. Find a comfy chair, kick back, explore Droid's user interface, and try some apps. Sometimes, the best way to learn is to do things yourself, so plan to taking some time off to practice during each chapter, and you'll get the hang of the Android operating system in no time.

When you've got the hang of the user interface and have become a touchscreen Jedi, you'll be ready to turn your attention to the software that makes the Droid the amazing device that it is. That software is the topic of Chapter 3.

3

Droid Software

Bringing a smartphone to market isn't trivial, and making it a commercial success is even harder. It takes a special combination of software, hardware, carriers, and willing consumers to turn a smartphone into a commercial success.

In this chapter, I explore one of the critical links in that chain: the Android operating system. Google has developed an amazing portfolio of free Web applications (like Gmail and Google Docs), so it only makes sense that it would bring that experience to smartphones.

I explore all the major areas of Android, including the home screen, status bar, and notifications, and round out the chapter with apps and widgets. Knowing the basic building blocks will help you get the most out of your Droid.

Touring the Home Screen

Welcome home. I've been expecting you.

Think of the Android home screen (**Figure 3.1**) as your desk: It's where you organize and use your apps in a way that's most effective for you. Touch something to open it; touch the Home key to return home.

Figure 3.1

The default Android 2.2 home screen on the Droid Pro. (Your model may be slightly different.)

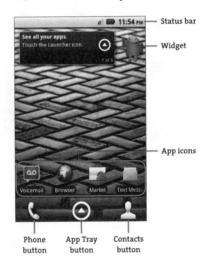

— Status bar

— Widget

— App icons

Phone button   App Tray button   Contacts button

Popular destinations are easy to get to thanks to the shortcuts on your home screen. Touch the Browser shortcut to surf the Web, or touch the Phone button to make a call. For a fun diversion, touch the circle-and-triangle icon at the bottom of the home screen to reveal the app tray, which lists all the apps on your Droid.

tip When you open an app or widget for the first time, touch its Menu key to see options for that particular app.

Going home

The primary home screen is where you'll land whenever you press the Home key on the bottom of your Droid. I say *primary* because your Droid actually has seven (count 'em!) home screens (**Figure 3.2**).

Figure 3.2 *A bird's-eye view of Android's seven home screens.*

The easiest way to figure out where you are is to remember that home is actually screen No. 4, smack in the middle of your seven home screens. When you drag a finger horizontally across the screen, you'll find three more home screens to the right and three more to the left. This arrangement gives you plenty of space to store frequently used app shortcuts and leaves a bunch of real estate for widgets (which I cover later in this chapter).

tip   These secondary home screens are great for storing shortcuts and widgets that you use less frequently or that don't quite make the cut to the big leagues.

Because you land on the home screen after pressing the convenient Home key, you should dedicate that screen to shortcuts for your most frequently used apps. Out of the box, Google places several of the most commonly used apps on the home screen (including Voicemail, Browser, Market, and Text Messages), along with a help widget: the chatty Android mascot that you see across the top of Figure 3.1.

Customizing your home screen

The best feature of the Droid home screen is that it's completely customizable. Touch and hold an icon, and you'll feel a short vibration indicating that you can now move that app to any of the seven home screens. Touch and hold an empty space to add a shortcut or widget to a home screen. My Android home screen is very dynamic, as I continually shuffle and shift apps between pages.

Viewing the app tray

One shortcut on the home screen worth noting is the icon that looks like a circle with a triangle in the center, smack-dab in the bottom middle of your home screen (refer to Figure 3.1). Touching that icon exposes the *app tray*—a scrolling list of all the apps installed on your Droid (**Figure 3.3**).

Figure 3.3
The app tray is home to your Droid's apps.

Apps are sorted alphabetically, and you scroll through them vertically by flicking upward or downward anywhere inside the window. You can launch an app from the drawer by touching it or (on Droids with keyboards, like the Droid 2 and Pro; refer to Chapter 1) by pressing the Return key.

I discuss apps in much more detail in Chapter 9, which covers the Android Market.

Navigating the Status Bar

Another defining feature of Android is the ingenious status bar permanently affixed to the top of the screen (**Figure 3.4**). Think of the status bar as being a clearinghouse for all the alerts, messages, alarms, and other notifications you could possibly receive on a mobile device . . . and then some.

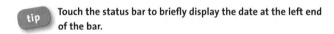

Figure 3.4 *Android's status bar is one of its most useful features.*

> **tip**　Touch the status bar to briefly display the date at the left end of the bar.

The status bar is rather small, so it can be hard to discern icons and symbols, especially some of the less common ones. (I provide a chart of common notification icons in the following section.) You can pull down the status bar by touching it and dragging down without lifting your finger. This drag reveals a resizable (up to full-screen) display of all your current status notifications and more information about each one, such as your number of unread emails. Touching any of these extended notifications takes you directly to the application that produced it so that you can listen to the voicemail or read the text message, for example.

Touching the Clear button in the top-right corner of the screen removes the status notifications that can clutter the status bar. It's amazing how many notifications Android can generate, especially if you receive a lot of email and text messages—and if you're a user of social networks like Twitter and Facebook, be prepared to be inundated by notifications. The Clear button will come in handy plenty of times. (I cover notifications in detail in the next section.)

The status bar is available to every application that you download, so be prepared to see all kinds of new icons pop up in it from time to time. Luckily, almost every application allows you to choose how you receive its notifications. If your status bar is getting cluttered with alerts, like the one in **Figure 3.5**, touch the Menu button when you're in the offending application; then find the setting to change the way that the app notifies you. Good apps offer many notification options; bad ones don't (and sometimes make it hard to find the notification settings at all).

Figure 3.5 *An example of status-bar overload. You need a vacation, my friend.*

Knowing Your Notifications

Notifications are integral parts of the Android ecosystem. They're used generously by both the operating system and by third-party apps. When you know your Droid's notification icons, you'll be able to glean a lot of information at a glance.

Figure 3.6 shows a chart of the most common notification icons and their meanings. Most of these icons are self-explanatory; others, not so much.

Figure 3.6
*The standard
Android
notification icons.*

🔵	Bluetooth active	📶	network (full signal)
📍	GPS active	📶	network (roaming)
📶	Wi-Fi active	**3G**	3G (fastest data)
🔵	downloading	✈	airplane mode
📳	vibrate	🔄	sync active
🔕	silent	⏰	alarm set
📵	mute call	🔋	battery (charging)
🔇	speakerphone active	🔋	battery (full charge)

MOTOROLA MOBILITY, INC.

Managing Apps

Such a wealth of apps is available for Android—more than 200,000 apps at last count—that you'll eventually need to get rid of some. Whether you don't use an app anymore, an app misbehaves, or you just plain need to free some space, it's a good idea to periodically prune the apps installed on your Droid.

To remove (or *uninstall*) an app, simply follow these steps:

1. Launch the Android Market app (see Chapter 9).

2. Touch the Menu button.

3. Touch My Apps.

4. Touch the app you want to remove.

5. Touch the Uninstall button in the app's screen (**Figure 3.7** on the next page).

Figure 3.7

You can uninstall (or update) an app easily from within the Android Market.

Alternatively, you can manage any app installed on your Droid by navigating to Settings > Apps > Manage Applications and then touching the app in question. A detailed app-info screen opens, displaying a prominent Uninstall button in the top-right corner (**Figure 3.8**). This method can be helpful if you want to uninstall or force-stop an app that's misbehaving, which sometimes happens after an update.

Figure 3.8

You can also uninstall and force-stop apps from within the settings app.

You can also reduce the amount of space that an app is using by touching the Clear Data button in the app-info screen. In addition, you can save space in your Droid's internal memory by moving some apps (and their data) to your SD card, although this method doesn't work for all apps.

When you want to remove an app or widget from the home screen (and trust me, this will happen), simply touch and hold its icon. When you do, the circle-and-triangle icon on the app tray turns into a trash can. (I cover the app tray at the end of the chapter.) Then just drag the app over the trash can to remove it from your home screen. The icon and the trash can glow red when they touch, confirming the deletion (**Figure 3.9**).

Figure 3.9
Not that you'd ever do it or anything, but this is how you'd remove Angry Birds from a home screen. You know, in theory.

 Dragging to the trash doesn't delete the app itself from your phone; it deletes just the shortcut (or alias) from your home screen.

Working with Widgets

First it was applications, and then just apps, and now widgets reduce software's footprint even further. Widgets (**Figure 3.10**) are miniature apps that run on the Android home screen—as opposed to just sitting there idly, like they do on the iPhone. The primary benefit of widgets is that they run in the background and can display useful information on your home screen without any intervention.

Figure 3.10

News, weather, social, and toggle widgets are the most popular types.

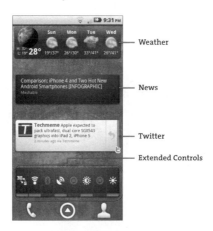

Weather

News

Twitter

Extended Controls

Widgets are insanely useful because they receive and display periodic updates, such as weather forecasts, unread email, upcoming appointments, and every kind of clock and alarm imaginable. You can use them to keep tabs on stock prices, sports scores, and even the price of gold. Widgets are also fast, because you don't have to touch an app and then wait for it to launch before completing your task.

Widgets can display battery, memory, and other system information on the home screen, and a whole class of switch widgets lets you toggle features like 3G/4G, Wi-Fi, Bluetooth, and GPS to save battery life. One example is Extended Controls (refer to Figure 3.10), which I discuss in "Battery Conservation 101" later in this chapter.

In addition, widgets are especially useful if you use social-networking services like Twitter and Facebook, because they can display your current timeline or wall right on your home screen and allow you to check in with one touch.

Music-discovery widgets like Shazam are quite handy because they launch quickly, allowing you to capture just enough of a song to identify it before it ends. Music-player widgets allow you to play, pause, skip, and otherwise control your music right from the home screen without launching an app.

Widgets are especially handy for one-touch operations, like touching a flashlight widget to instantly turn the LED flash into a flashlight. A smartphone flashlight is amazingly convenient, especially during the dark winter months, so that's one widget that's always on my primary home screen.

Managing Battery Life

Unfortunately, manufacturers' battery-life estimate are perfect-world numbers that are used to market the phone and don't reflect typical real-world use. (In manufacturers' defense, battery life is extremely hard to quantify and benchmark because everyone uses devices differently.)

Battery consumption

Your Droid's battery consumption depends on several factors, most of which are common sense:

- **Radio use.** A smartphone's *radios*—transmitters and receivers—are major consumers of battery power, and a Droid has lots of radios.

Depending on the model you own, your Droid may include radios for 3G or 4G, GPS, Wi-Fi, Bluetooth, and CDMA.

- **Phone activity.** Phone calls use battery power, so the more calls you make and take, the less time your battery will last.

- **Screen brightness and timeout settings.** It takes a lot of power to light up a Droid's large screen. Keeping the phone on longer than necessary, and keeping the screen brighter than necessary, will consume more battery power.

- **Camera use.** Droid's 5- to 8-megapixel camera (depending on your model) has as much horsepower as many point-and-shoot digital cameras, which is a drain on the battery. Taking pictures will reduce your battery life somewhat, but taking videos will reduce your battery even faster.

For tips on getting the most life out of your battery, read on.

Battery Conservation 101

High-tech smartphones with lots of power-hungry radios can chew through a charged battery pack before the clock strikes noon. Implementing a couple of the following management and conservation techniques can make your battery go the extra mile:

- **Change your Extended Controls settings.** You can extend the Droid's battery life with the Extended Controls widget (refer to "Working with Widgets" earlier in this chapter), which makes it easy to toggle such power-hungry settings as Wi-Fi, Bluetooth, GPS, data syncing, and screen brightness. Install it from the home screen by touching Menu > Add > Widgets > Extended Controls.

- **Turn off features that you don't use.** If you don't regularly use Wi-Fi, Bluetooth, or GPS, turn them off in Settings or via the Extended Controls widget (see the preceding item). If you don't need any connectivity, turn on airplane mode (touch Settings > Wireless & Networks).

- **Keep the screen at the lowest brightness that you can tolerate.** To adjust the brightness, touch Settings > Sound & Display, and scroll down to the bottom of the list. The same goes for the screen timeout setting: Keep it at 1 minute, and turn the screen off when you're not using it by touching the End button.

- **Disable autosync if you don't need real-time email.** Touch Settings > Accounts & Sync; then clear the Background Data and Auto-Sync check boxes. Deselecting Background Data stops apps from syncing and sending/receiving data. Deselecting Auto-Sync stops the Droid from syncing data (email, calendar events, and contacts) automatically.

- **Use shortcuts for frequently used apps.** Using shortcuts (touch Settings > Apps > Quick Launch) saves screen touches and scrolls, and shortens the amount of time that the screen is on.

- **Install new firmware updates on your phone shortly after they're released.** Firmware updates almost always improve battery life in addition to adding features and fixing bugs. To check whether you're due for a system update, touch Settings > About Phone > Status > System Updates.

tip An application called Locale, which is available in the Android Market for $9.99, can manage almost every aspect of a Droid dynamically, including neat things such as automatically switching to your home Wi-Fi network when it's in range and turning off 3G and GPS. For details, see the Locale Web site (www.twofortyfouram.com). I cover third-party apps and the Android Market in Chapter 9.

Now that you've had a chance to look at the Google software that makes the Droid tick, it's time to dig a little deeper into the technology—specifically, the Droid's hardware and all those power-hungry radios. Turn the page to Chapter 4.

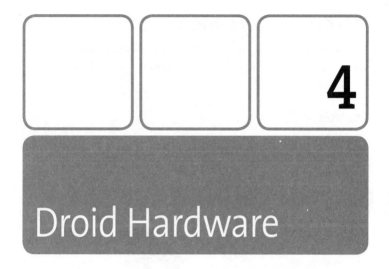

4

Droid Hardware

In this chapter, I dig into a few of the Droid's key hardware features, including the keyboard, battery, memory card, and *radios*—the chips that the Droid uses for sending and receiving data. For the most part, the radios work silently in the background, but learning how to control them can save you battery life for important things (like playing Angry Birds).

The Droid's hardware by its very nature can be a tad technical at times. If you're not a hardware person, feel free to jump around a bit or turn to a chapter that covers one of the more entertaining aspects of your Droid (such as software or apps).

Hardware Keys and Controls

To fully realize the potential of your Droid, it's important to master the various hardware controls and interface elements that make all the magic happen.

Controls

Figure 4.1 gives you a close look at the controls and keys on the Droid Bionic oriented vertically (also called portrait mode). The Bionic is the newest member of the Droid family and features several firsts, such as two CPU cores and a 4G radio, so I tend to favor it in the screen shots in this book.

Figure 4.1
Droid Bionic.

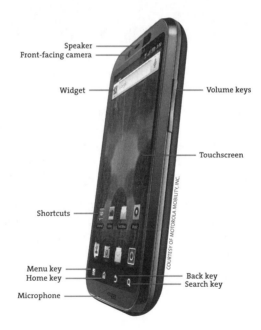

The hardware keys on the various Droids are similar, so I review them more generally in the following sections. For specifics on your particular model, refer to "The Droids You're Looking For" in Chapter 1.

Home-row keys

Every Droid has a row of hardware keys along the bottom of the screen (**Figure 4.2**). These home-row keys are integral parts of the Android experience, allowing you to access the menu and search features easily, but they're most useful as ripcords when you need to go home or back—stat!

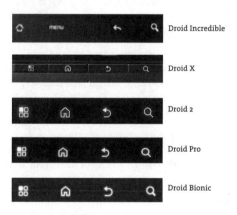

Figure 4.2
Five Droid models' Home keys compared. Which one doesn't belong?

Droid Incredible

Droid X

Droid 2

Droid Pro

Droid Bionic

One problem with Android phones is that hardware manufacturers have been known to take a few liberties with their designs. Witness Figure 4.2, which displays the home-row keys on five Droid models. Notice anything different? Yes, the Droid Incredible (pictured at the top of Figure 4.2) has swapped Home and Menu keys compared with the rest of the Droids. What's the reason for this swap? The Motorola Droids (X, 2, Pro, and Bionic) have the same home-row key configuration, but the Incredible is manufactured by HTC Corp., which has a slightly different opinion from Motorola about where the keys belong.

In the following sections, I take a look at the four very important keys that comprise the home row on a Droid.

Hardware vs. Capacitive Keys

Notice anything *else* different in Figure 4.2? Yup, the Droid X (second from the top) has *hardware* home keys—that is, physical keys that click when you press them. The other four Droids use *capacitive* keys, which react to the touch of your finger just like the touchscreen does. Capacitive sensors detect anything that is conductive or has dielectric properties. (A *dielectric* is an electrical insulator that can be polarized by an applied electrical field.)

One advantage of the hardware keys on the Droid X is that you can wake the device just by pressing the Home key. The X model is the only Droid that supports this feature. The only way to wake a Droid that has capacitive buttons is to press the Sleep/Wake button (usually located along the top edge).

Personally, I prefer real hardware keys to the newer capacitive keys. There's just something special about the tactile response of real keys, which move and click when you press them, providing valuable feedback to the user.

Even with *haptic* feedback (that slight vibrating buzz that you hear when you touch the screen), a capacitive key is no replacement for a real key; it doesn't provide any feedback to the user when pressed; and it's much easier to touch accidentally. Capacitive keys are less expensive to manufacture and don't break as often because they use no moving parts—two great reasons for hardware makers to choose them over more-expensive, breakable hardware keys.

Back

A unique feature of the Droid—one that's not available on the iPhone—is the Back key (refer to Figure 4.2). As you'd expect, it takes you back to the last screen that you viewed. In fact, the Back key operates exactly like the Web-browser Back button that you've come to know and love.

The Back key also functions like the Escape (or Esc) key on a standard computer keyboard, in that it dismisses dialog boxes and the menu interface. If you want to get out of where you are but don't necessarily want to go home, the Back key is for you.

Menu

The Menu key (refer to Figure 4.2) is extremely useful in Android and isn't available on other popular phones. Pressing it displays a small overlay at the bottom of the screen (**Figure 4.3**), listing actions that are available in the current application. The Menu key is *contextual,* meaning that it presents different options depending on which app you're in. Usually, you can press it to find the various settings for a given application. (For more information on third-party applications, see Chapter 9.)

Figure 4.3
Pressing the Menu key presents five options.

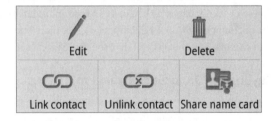

If you long-press the Menu key, the text labels below each option display their keyboard equivalents. (Search becomes Menu+S, for example.)

People who use the keyboard a lot or simply are faster at typing sometimes prefer keyboard shortcuts to key presses.

Pressing the Menu key also unlocks the phone after the screen timeout interval (which you set by touching Settings > Sound & Display) has elapsed.

Home

The Home key (refer to Figure 4.2) is equally intuitive. Pressing it takes you . . . well, home. It's a nice escape hatch from the depths of your Droid and a simple way to find your way back after an adventure through its various settings, menus, and applications.

tip Long-press the Home key to bring up a list of your most recently used applications. It's super-handy for switching between apps and functions, just like Command-Tab (Mac) or Alt+Tab (Windows).

Search

Because search is a core feature of Android and the Droid phones, it's a perfectly logical choice for a hardware key. Press the Search key to bring up the Quick Search box. Then you can type your search keyword or touch the microphone icon and begin speaking. For more information on the Quick Search box and voice search, see the "Search" section in Chapter 1.

Keyboards (Droid 2 and Droid Pro)

The hardware QWERTY keyboards on the Droid 2 and Droid Pro are what differentiate those models from other Droids. Users who rely on their phones to send email and/or text messages regularly already know the value of a QWERTY keyboard and may even have purchased a Droid 2 or Pro just for this reason.

The Droid 2 (**Figure 4.4**) features a horizontal slide-out keyboard.
Although the Droid is completely operable via its touchscreen with the
keyboard concealed, many people prefer to use the hardware keyboard
for texting and for composing email.

Figure 4.4
*The Droid 2,
oriented
horizontally with
its keyboard
extended.*

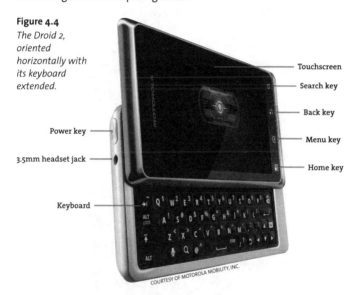

Touchscreen

Search key

Back key

Power key

Menu key

3.5mm headset jack

Home key

Keyboard

COURTESY OF MOTOROLA MOBILITY, INC.

The original Droid keyboard was universally panned by users, so Motorola
listened to the feedback and improved the Droid 2 keyboard 100 percent.
It's much more tactile and has more travel and separation between the
keys, and you'll be able to type on it pretty quickly with a little practice.
This improvement is another example of how much things have changed
in the world of Android in a year.

The Droid Pro (**Figure 4.5**) has a vertical keyboard permanently located below the touchscreen. If the Pro looks eerily similar to the iconic BlackBerry, that's no accident. Research In Motion (RIM) has long had the top phone in the smartphone market, and now that Android has conquered Apple's iOS, it's gunning for the No. 1 spot.

Figure 4.5
The Droid Pro's fixed vertical keyboard is the spitting image of the BlackBerry keyboard.

Power key — Headset jack
Notification LED
Volume keys — Programmable key
Touchscreen
Home key — Back key
Menu key — Search key
Micro USB port —
Microphone —

MOTOROLA MOBILITY, INC.

Battery

Each Droid comes with a rechargeable lithium-ion battery that typically allows you to talk for approximately 8 hours or keep the phone on standby for more than 10 days. Your Droid's battery consumption depends on several factors, most of which are common sense, including mobile broadband (4G) use, number of calls made, screen brightness, radio use, and camera use. For more tips on getting the most life out of your battery, refer to "Managing Battery Life" in Chapter 3.

Although the Droid's battery (shown removed in **Figure 4.6**) is much better than that of previous Android phones, manufacturer battery specs are rarely achieved in real-world use. The good news is that with a moderate amount of conservation, you can expect to get a full day's use out of the included battery.

Figure 4.6 *Rear view of the Droid Pro with the SIM card, microSD card, and battery removed.*

Battery charge

When you first start your Droid, the included battery can have anything from zero charge to a partial charge. Assuming that you don't have to run out the door with it right now or anything, I recommend connecting your phone to the wall charger to give it a good solid charge.

note The Droid is always on—and can't be turned off—when it's being charged. Luckily, you can still black the screen by pressing the Power key.

You should fully charge the Droid's battery before using the phone. Depending on how much charge remains, a recharge should take about 1.5 to 2 hours. I don't know about you, but there's almost no chance that I'll put down a new gadget long enough to charge it fully. I recommend that you find a comfy chair next to an outlet, plug in the Droid, and explore a bit while it charges for the first time.

Like most Android-powered phones, the Droid comes with a lithium-ion (abbreviated *li-ion*) battery. This battery doesn't suffer from the memory effect, in that you don't have to drain it completely before recharging it. I still try to fully charge my Droid's battery whenever possible, but this practice is mostly habit (and partly superstition?) and isn't necessary.

Charging methods

You have two ways to charge your Droid's battery:

- **Charger cable.** The charger cable came in the box with your phone. You've probably charged devices with a cable like this since you were 5 years old, so I'll let you figure that one out yourself. You can find the Micro USB charging port on an edge of your Droid.

- **USB port.** The alternative is to plug your phone into an available USB port on a computer, using the included USB cable. This method is a boon if you travel with a notebook computer because you can leave the bulky brick at home and charge your phone simply by connecting it to your notebook via USB.

USB Charging

To charge the Droid via USB, make sure that the host computer is awake—that is, not in sleep or hibernate mode. Most computers turn off their USB ports while they're sleeping, which will prevent your Droid from charging.

A computer's USB port outputs 500 mA (the official USB specification), which will charge your Droid slower than the included AC adapter (which outputs between 850 mA and 1000 mA).

Charging schedule

Your charging schedule depends on how you use your Droid. If you're a casual user who places and receives fewer than ten calls per day and uses the phone's Internet features sparingly, I recommend that you charge your phone each night while you sleep. Although the phone may not need a charge at the end of each day, charging nightly is a hedge against the chance that you'll have an unexpectedly busy day tomorrow and your phone will run out of juice just when you need it most.

If you're a heavy user of features such as 4G, GPS, and Wi-Fi, you can literally watch the battery meter trickle down as you use your Droid, and you need to plan accordingly. Heavy users may have a tough time making it through a standard business day on a fully charged battery. If this sounds like you, you'll want to read the next section and "Managing Battery Life" in Chapter 3.

note **Micro USB is the small flat port on your Droid where you connect the charger. It's now an industry standard, which means that you'll have an easier time finding a charger in a pinch.**

Backup batteries

As I mention earlier in this chapter, Droids eat batteries for lunch, and even a moderate user will eventually need a backup battery. Luckily, replacement batteries are relatively cheap—around $40 for a new Motorola Droid—which makes purchasing one a no-brainer. Do yourself a favor: Pick up an extra battery, and keep it in your gear bag.

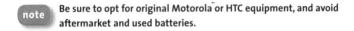

note Be sure to opt for original Motorola or HTC equipment, and avoid aftermarket and used batteries.

tip Charge and rotate the batteries often. Batteries of this type lose about 10 percent of their charge per month and discharge completely before you know it.

If you want even more power, you can purchase a battery with double the capacity (as high as 2600 mAh) of the Droid's original battery for less than $50 on the aftermarket. Although it effectively doubles your Droid's run time, this type of battery requires a replacement rear cover to cover the extra bulge. Think in terms of a trade-off: You can have longer run time if you're willing to add some size and weight in exchange.

note If you're a heavy user, you can purchase additional stock batteries or extended-life batteries from sites such as www.seidioonline.com.

Memory Card

A great feature of the Droid (and most other Android phones) is the included expansion-card slot, which allows you an infinite amount of expansion beyond what's available internally for app storage. Expansion cards have unlimited uses and capacity, and you can add as many cards as you need. The expansion-card slot is a key feature that's not available in the iPhone.

The expansion-card slot on the Droid accepts Micro SDHC (Micro Secure Digital High Capacity) cards, which are even smaller than the SD cards used in many digital cameras. Micro SDHC (which the industry has shortened to microSD) memory cards are just a hair over half an inch on their longest side and are easy to lose, so keep them in a safe place.

The microSD card slot on the Droid is typically located on the bottom of the phone in the battery compartment (**Figure 4.7**). To access it, you sometimes have to remove the battery first—which shuts down the phone. Plan ahead: First shut the Droid down gracefully by pressing and holding the Power key and then touching Power Off.

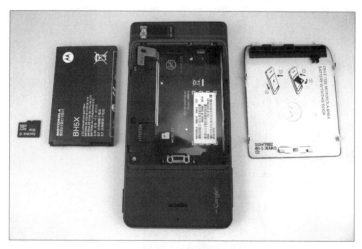

Figure 4.7 *The Droid X with its battery and Micro SD card removed.*

Droids support microSD cards up to 32 GB, but the 16 GB card that comes preinstalled should be more than adequate for most users. If you need additional storage, you can purchase more 16 GB cards for around $20 each; 32 GB cards sell for around $65 each.

Due to Moore's Law (which I define in the following note) and the dynamics of book publishing, there's a good chance that 64 GB or even 128 GB microSD cards could be available by the time you read this book. Before you buy such a card, make sure that the Android operating system (OS) you're running supports the larger card. A 32 GB card is a waste if your phone recognizes only 16 GB of it.

note Moore's Law describes a trend in the history of computing hardware in which the number of transistors on an integrated circuit doubles approximately every 2 years.

note The SDHC standard goes only to 32 GB, but the SD Association has approved a next-generation SDXC memory-card specification that's capable of storing up to 2 TB.

When a card is installed in the Droid, you can unmount it, format it, and view its available storage by touching Settings > SD Card & Phone Storage (**Figure 4.8**).

Figure 4.8
*The SD Card &
Phone Storage
Settings screen.*

Radios

Before I get started discussing the Droid's various radios, I'm going to give you an overview of the acronyms associated with mobile technology. Unfortunately, alphabet soup comes with the territory.

Wireless acronyms

Tables 4.1 and 4.2 list some of the common acronyms used to represent the various types of data connections, network speeds, and network acronyms.

Table 4.1 Speed Acronyms

ACRONYM	MEANING
Kbps (Kilobits per second)	1,000 bits transferred over a 1-second period
Mbps (Megabits per second)	1,000,000 bits transferred over a 1-second period
Gbps (Gigabits per second)	1,000,000,000 bits transferred over a 1-second period

Table 4.2 Network Acronyms

ACRONYM	MEANING
2G/2.5G (Second generation, GPRS)	The 2.5G telecommunications hardware standard is a stepping stone between 2G and 3G that's capable of producing download speeds of 50–100 Kbps.
3G (Third generation)	This telecommunications hardware standards is capable of generating data throughput of up to 14 Mbps (download) and 5.8 Mbps (upload). See CDMA2000 later in this table.
4G (Fourth generation)	The 4G telecommunications hardware standard is capable of generating data throughput of 100 Mbps (down) and 30 Mbps (up) while moving and a screaming 1 Gbps (down) while stationary.
CDMA (Code Division Multiple Access)	CDMA is a shortened version of CDMA 2000.
CDMA2000 (Code Division Multiple Access 2000)	This family of 3G mobile technology standards, based on CDMA, is used to send voice and data between mobile phones and cell sites. All Droids run on Verizon's CDMA2000 network in the United States.
EV-DO (Evolution-Data Optimized)	This telecommunications standard for transmitting data wirelessly via radio signals is used primarily to access the Internet. It's part of the CDMA2000 family of standards and is frequently referred to as *3G data* or *mobile broadband.* EV-DO Rev. A is theoretically capable of generating download speeds of up to 3 Mbps, but in practice, you'll find speeds to be closer to 1 Mbps.

(continues)

Table 4.2 Network Acronyms (continued)

Acronym	Meaning
GPRS (General Packet Radio Service)	GPRS is a packet-oriented mobile data service used on both 2G and 3G GSM networks.
GPS (Global Positioning System)	GPS satellites help your phone calculate its longitude and latitude; then the phone uses this information to pinpoint your location on a map. I review all kinds of other cool stuff that GPS does later in this chapter.
GSM (Global System for Mobile communications)	GSM is a 2G system used by more than 80 percent of the mobile market. GSM also pioneered Short Message Service (SMS), which has been adopted by most phone carriers worldwide.
LTE (Long Term Evolution)	LTE, the successor to CDMA2000, is marketed by Verizon Wireless as 4G. It's more accurate, however, to call LTE "pre-4G" or "3.9G" because it delivers download speeds of only 10–30 Mbps—a fraction of the 100–1000 Mbps speeds defined in the 4G specification.
LTE Advanced (Long Term Evolution Advanced)	LTE Advanced is a preliminary mobile communication standard that will be finalized in 2011. Hailed by users as true 4G, it represents the pinnacle of Internet access, with a peak data rate of 1 Gbps (1,000 Mbps) stationary and 100 Mbps while moving, as well as improved power management.

(continues)

Table 4.2 Network Acronyms (continued)

ACRONYM	MEANING
UMTS (Universal Mobile Telecommunications System)	This 3G mobile communication technology borrows and builds on GSM concepts. Currently, it's morphing into a 4G technology capable of producing even faster data-transfer rates.
Wi-Fi (Wireless fidelity)	If 4G isn't available, Wi-Fi usually is the next-fastest Internet access option. Speeds vary widely, depending on the wireless access point you're connected to. I cover Wi-Fi in detail later in this chapter.

Wireless standards

It's important to understand the differences between the two major tele-communications hardware standards. Although many other standards exist (see Table 4.2 in the preceding section), 3G and 4G are dominant in the United States, so 3G and 4G smartphones are the primary flavors.

4G

4G devices use the latest wireless radio and antenna technology to deliver blistering fast Internet speeds—up to 10 times faster than 3G—and are truly the next generation of mobile-phone technology. As they began hitting the market at the beginning of 2011, 4G devices running on the Verizon LTE network have been clocking download speeds as fast as 20–30 Mbps. That's *fast!* It shames my home Internet connection, which pokes along at around 8–10 Mbps down.

note Although LTE (used in the Droid Bionic) is marketed as 4G, first-release LTE doesn't fully comply with 4G requirements. LTE would be more accurately described as "pre-4G," as it's only a step toward LTE Advanced— a true 4G standard.

Fast data connections make things like videoconferencing and HD video streaming possible. 4G networks are so fast that you can download a song in 4 seconds and upload a photo in 6 seconds—about ten times faster than the best 3G connections available.

The Droid Bionic is the first member of the Android family to ship with so-called 4G technology, but soon, most high-end phones sold will be 4G.

The two downsides of 4G technology are build-out and power consumption. At this writing (February 2011), Verizon Wireless is offering LTE coverage in only 38 of the largest cities in the United States (including San Francisco; Washington, D.C.; and Philadelphia) and in 60 major airports. Verizon says that LTE will cover 110 million people in 2011 and that by the end of 2013, 4G will be available everywhere the company has 3G now.

Because they require more power, 4G radios consume more power than 3G radios do, making battery life an issue. Vigilant battery conservation (see "Managing Battery Life" in Chapter 3) is necessary to get the most run time out of next-generation 4G smartphones like the Bionic. Luckily, battery conservation in the Android OS has improved with the hardware, allowing most users to make it through a full day on a charge by using modest conservation settings.

 tip To see whether your area has Verizon's 4G/LTE coverage, visit http://network4g.verizonwireless.com.

3G

Because 4G is relatively new, most Droid use 3G telecommunications hardware standards. As you might expect, 3G devices are faster than

2G devices but slower than 4G devices (refer to Table 4.2 earlier in this chapter).

The biggest advantage that 3G has over 2G—or, more accurately, 2.5G—is faster wireless data. Apps that stream audio and video (including Pandora and Netflix) are the greatest beneficiaries of faster download speeds. Because 3G is capable of moving data faster than 2G is, the Internet feels faster on a 3G phone. Sites load faster, and audio and video play more smoothly.

Theoretically, 3G is capable of downloading data at 14 Mbps. In practice, it generates download speeds of about 1–3 Mbps, which is still much faster than the lowly 2.5G standard that it replaces. 2.5G can muster only around 50–100 Kbps down, can barely stream audio, and can't stream video at all.

Wireless coverage

Like anything that involves sending and receiving data, coverage can vary. Location, demand, structures, hardware, and software affect the signal quality and strength that your device gets. Also, as you'd expect, data coverage can vary widely by city and carrier.

You can check your carrier's data coverage by going to its Web site and searching for a coverage map. The four major U.S. carriers—Verizon, AT&T, T-Mobile, and Sprint—maintain coverage maps on their Web sites.

Be forewarned, though: Don't take a coverage map at face value. Just because the coverage map says your area is covered by a given network doesn't mean that it actually is. Because many variables can affect coverage, it's best to test the quality of the network before signing any long-term contract.

One easy way to do this is to borrow a friend's device that operates on the carrier in question. Vigorously test the quality of the voice and data network in the locations where you're going to use your device most—typically, at home and at work. Stress-test it by placing and receiving numerous calls and by streaming high-definition audio and video on the device at different times of day. Odds are pretty good that if the network is up to stuff on your friend's device, it'll work acceptably for you too.

Testing isn't a guarantee, however. This type of test doesn't take into account changes in hardware and software if you're getting a different device from your friend's.

note Another reason to test a network is the total cost of ownership of a Droid over a 2-year contract, which falls between $2,800 and $3,800. Considering the cost, it's critical to do your homework before signing on the dotted line.

If, after purchasing your Droid, you discover that your coverage isn't acceptable, don't fret. Verizon Wireless allows you to terminate service within 30 days of activation—for any reason.

Wireless technology

CDMA (Code Division Multiple Access) is one of the two main competing network technologies for mobile phones in the United States. The other is GSM (Global System for Mobile communications). In this section, I cover both technologies.

note GSM networks continue to make inroads in the United States, and CDMA networks make progress in other parts of the world. Each camp firmly believes that its preferred architecture is superior to the other.

CDMA2000

CDMA2000, based on CDMA, is a mobile-technology standard that's popular in North America and parts of Asia. It's used to send voice and data between mobile phones and cell sites.

As of 2009, 308 operators in 116 countries offered CDMA2000 networks, including several in rapidly growing markets like China and India, pushing worldwide subscribers to more than half a billion people. More than 25 percent of those subscribers are EV-DO (mobile broadband) users. Major CDMA carriers in the United States include Sprint PCS, Verizon, and Virgin Mobile.

There are two types of CDMA2000:

- **1x.** Also known as 1x and 1xRTT (or *1 times Radio Transmission Technology*), 1x is the first and most basic CDMA2000 wireless standard. The standard supports packet data speeds of up to 153 Kbps, with real-world data averages between 60 Kbps and 100 Kbps.

- **1xEV-DO.** EV-DO is a wireless telecommunications standard designed specifically for the transmission of data. Faster than straight 1x, 1xEV-DO has a theoretical downstream rate of 2 Mbps and real-world download speeds of 300–700 Kbps, which is comparable to basic DSL.

    A faster version of EV-DO called *Revision A* or just *Rev. A* is capable of supporting data rates of 3.1 Mbps down and 1.8 Mbps up, although 1 Mbps down and 500 Kbps up are more realistic.

Actual download and upload speeds are based on a variety of factors, which I cover earlier in this chapter, so your mileage may vary.

GSM

GSM is a 2G mobile-phone system that's the primary competitor of CDMA. Like CDMA (which is used in the Droid), GSM sends voice and data between mobile phones and cell sites; unlike CDMA, it's used by more than 1.5 billion people in more than 212 countries and territories, outnumbering CDMA by a large margin.

Wi-Fi

The stratospheric growth of the Internet is directly related to the proliferation of wireless technology. In the not-too-distant past (before 1999 or so), accessing the Internet meant sitting down in front of a computer with an Ethernet or RJ11 cable plugged into a jack on the wall. The wires went only so far, though, and users were forced to step away from the computer to do things like dress, walk down the street, and drive to work.

Well, no more. The invention of the wireless router and a funny protocol called 802.11b allowed us to access data from as much as 300 feet away—without wires. Wi-Fi, as it became known, was a huge contributor to the rapid rise of the Internet.

Wi-Fi was a definite tipping point for technology at the turn of the century, liberating us from the shackles of the cables and wires that previously bound us our desks. Today, it's easier than ever to use an inexpensive wireless router to surf the Internet from the couch, kitchen, or bedroom with ease. Now that wireless Internet access is everywhere (or so it seems), many gadgets come with wireless radios built in.

Android-powered Droids are no exceptions. In fact, Wi-Fi is a bona fide requirement for a smartphone these days. Consumers simply won't buy a smartphone if it can't connect to their Wi-Fi networks at home and at work. (In November 2008, RIM and Verizon Wireless released the original BlackBerry Storm *without* Wi-Fi, and it was universally panned by critics, including me.)

Using Wi-Fi

Like most things on the Droid, Wi-Fi isn't very complicated to set up. Just touch Settings > Wireless & Networks to set up everything you need to access a Wi-Fi network at your home or office. When Wi-Fi access is set up, your preferred wireless access points are stored on the Droid, so you can pretty much set it and forget it. Next time you're within range of a Wi-Fi access point that you've connected to before, the Droid will switch automatically from 3G to the faster Wi-Fi.

To connect to a Wi-Fi network, touch Settings > Wireless & Networks to open the Wireless & Network Settings screen (**Figure 4.9**); then touch Wi-Fi Settings. In the resulting Wi-Fi Settings screen (**Figure 4.10**), touch one of the networks listed in the Wi-Fi Networks section. Networks that are encrypted with a password (such as Galaxy in Figure 4.10) display a lock over the Wi-Fi icon and require you to enter a password to gain access. Open networks, which don't require a password, display the basic Wi-Fi icon sans lock.

Figure 4.9
*Wireless &
Network Settings
screen.*

Figure 4.10
*Wi-Fi Settings
screen.*

If you want to connect to a network that's not in the list, just touch Add
Wi-Fi Network at the bottom of the Wi-Fi Settings screen. In the resulting
screen (**Figure 4.11**), enter the network's Service Set ID (Network SSID),
choose an option from the Security drop-down menu, and enter a password as appropriate for that particular network; then touch Save.

Figure 4.11
*Adding a Wi-Fi
network.*

When you're connected to a Wi-Fi access point, you'll see a Wi-Fi icon in the status bar. (For a chart of the popular Android status-bar icons, flip back to Chapter 3.) The four segments in the icon indicate how strong your connection is. A Wi-Fi icon with a question mark over it indicates a problem with the wireless connection.

Surfing safely

To wrap up this section, I want to leave you with a little anecdote about Wi-Fi security. In short, don't trust unknown networks with your confidential information. It's trivial to create a network called Starbucks, Marriott, or Hilton Honors and then monitor the traffic of anyone who connects to it—a practice called *spoofing*. A spoofed network is designed to look and operate like a normal Wi-Fi network, with one nefarious difference: The person who set it up could be scanning the traffic flowing through it for potentially valuable information.

If you plop down in a comfy chair in your favorite coffee shop and connect to the first free wireless access point that pops up, you could be connected to the laptop of the guy next to you, and he could be capturing your login information as you access your online bank account.

Not all free wireless access points are set up by hackers to steal your information, mind you. My point is that you must use common sense when using unknown Wi-Fi networks. Surfing the Web is pretty safe on a wireless network, for example, but logging in to your email account can expose your login credentials to a bad guy. I'd refrain from logging in to any financial Web site (bank, credit union, investments, and so on) whatsoever while you're logged in to a Wi-Fi network that you don't know. It's just not worth the risk.

tip   **Change your passwords often, and use different passwords for different sites. Most people rarely change their passwords, and some use
the same password for all the Web sites they access. Does this sound like you?
You could be risking the security of your identity, because when bad guys have
your password, they can do a lot of damage with it. A friendly warning: Don't
be promiscuous in your wireless surfing habits.**

GPS

One of the most useful features of the Droid is its dedicated GPS hardware, which gives you access to the 24 to 32 GPS satellites circling over-
head. These satellites provide the Droid hyperaccurate positioning data
that previously was available only to the military.

GPS satellites broadcast signals from space, and GPS receivers like the
one in the Droid use those signals to provide three-dimensional location data (latitude, longitude, and altitude) and the precise time. The
heavy lifting is done on the handset itself, where apps like Google Maps
(Chapter 7) translate the longitude and latitude coordinates sent by the
satellites into a dot on a map representing your current location.

With an accuracy of 1 to 10 meters (depending on how many "birds"
you're locked onto), there's no denying that GPS is perfectly suited for
navigation. Its popularity is exploding as new smartphone apps designed
for GPS flow into the market.

You can turn the GPS feature on and off easily with a quick trip to the
handy Settings app. Simply navigate to Settings > Location & Security,
and check (or clear) the green boxes labeled Use GPS Satellites and
Enable Assisted GPS (**Figure 4.12** on the next page).

Figure 4.12

Settings that enable the GPS receiver are tucked away in the Location & Security Settings screen.

note The Use Wireless Networks setting just above the Use GPS Satellites setting allows your Droid to determine your location via the wireless networks around you. Be warned, though: Checking this box means that you consent to sending anonymous location data to Google, even while no apps are running.

If you're not a heavy user, I recommend keeping GPS on all the time, because it adds a new dimension of utility to your phone (as you see in this section) with almost no downside. But when you're using the Droid for real-time navigation, GPS is a major battery hog; in fact, it's one of the biggest battery consumers on the Droid.

A little common sense goes a long way here. If you're planning an all-day walk, hike, bike ride, or any other event that will have you away from power for an extended period, you should turn off all unnecessary radios (like GPS) unless you need them. When this feature isn't in use, the GPS chip goes into low-power mode, saving precious milliamps. (See my battery-conservation tips in Chapter 3.)

If you're a fan of automotive GPS receivers from Garmin, please check out my *Garmin nüvi Pocket Guide*, also from Peachpit Press.

Using GPS Creatively

The first and most common use of GPS technology is to get directions from point A to point B. It's an incredibly powerful feature that millions of people rely on every day to get to their destination. GPS is especially useful for getting directions on your Droid.

GPS isn't just for maps, though. Here's a sample of the fun location-based apps available for the Droid:

- **Layar** is a *reality browser,* which uses your Droid's camera, compass, and GPS to display real-time information about your surroundings on your Droid's screen over the live camera image.

- **Trapster** alerts you as you approach speed traps, red lights, traffic cameras, police checkpoints, accidents, and other road hazards.

- **Waze** is a community-driven, turn-by-turn navigation app that uses data from users' driving times to provide real-time traffic updates and optimal routing.

- **Where's My Droid** helps you locate your Droid if you misplace it with the ringer on mute. If you have this app installed and misplace your Droid, you can text it and get its GPS location. Brilliant! (I need an app like this for my car keys.)

All these apps are available for free in the Android Market, which I cover in detail in Chapter 9.

Bluetooth

Bluetooth—an open wireless protocol for exchanging data over short distances—seems to have been invented for mobile phones. Compared with 3G and Wi-Fi, which are designed primarily for Internet access, Bluetooth has a short range. Bluetooth 2.1 with Enhanced Data Rate (EDR) supports theoretical data transfer speeds of up to 3 Mbps at a range of about 33 feet, but you can expect more like 10 to 20 feet in the real world.

Like the other radios covered in this chapter, Bluetooth drains the Droid's battery quickly when it's enabled, although not as quickly as 4G, GPS, and Wi-Fi do. It's important to practice good conservation techniques and use Bluetooth sparingly when you're away from power for long stretches of time.

Bluetooth has many uses, such as creating personal area networks and sharing data between devices, but its primary application in mobile phones is wireless headsets. I cover various applications of Bluetooth in the following sections.

Headsets

Although they make us look like Borgs wandering around talking to ourselves, Bluetooth headsets have become part of the technology landscape. There's no denying the convenience of being able to talk to someone on a mobile phone completely hands-free; it expands the freedom that started with cordless phones at home. The difference, of course, is that instead of being able to wander around our houses yapping, now we can walk just about anywhere in the world yapping.

note If you don't have a Bluetooth headset, invest in a good one. Headsets from Jawbone.com are widely regarded as the best because of their military-grade-noise cancellation technology.

Setting up a Bluetooth headset in Android is simple. After you initially pair your headset and your Droid, the phone will remember the settings so that you don't have to repeat the pairing exercise each time you want to use your headset.

To get started, follow these steps:

1. Touch Settings > Wireless & Networks to display the Wireless & Network Settings screen, which includes Bluetooth and Bluetooth Settings options (**Figure 4.13**).

   You can tell at a glance whether Bluetooth is turned on; if it is, you'll see a check in its check box.

Figure 4.13
The Wireless & Network Settings screen is where you change Bluetooth settings.

2. If Bluetooth isn't turned on, touch the check box to enable it.

3. Touch the Bluetooth Settings option to open the Bluetooth Settings screen (**Figure 4.14**).

The Bluetooth Devices section of this screen is where all the action happens. Here, you'll see any Bluetooth devices that are within range of your phone and discoverable. If your headset isn't listed, make sure that it's in discoverable mode (if you're not sure how to do this, consult your headset's user manual for instructions) and then touch Menu > Scan for Devices.

Figure 4.14

The Bluetooth Settings screen is where you pair your Bluetooth devices.

4. When you see your headset in the Bluetooth Devices list (mine is called Jawbone ICON in Figure 4.14), touch it.

5. If you're prompted for a personal identification number (PIN) for your headset, enter that code to gain access to your device.

Consult your manual for your particular device's PIN, or search for it on Google.

 Many Bluetooth headsets that I've used have a PIN of 0000 or 1234, so if you're stuck, those codes are good places to start.

When Bluetooth is on, you'll see its blue icon in the status bar. For more information on status-bar icons, flip back to Chapter 3.

 Always use a wired or wireless headset when you use your phone while driving; in many states, it's the law.

Mind Your Mobile Manners

Although they have obvious safety benefits, such as allowing you to use a mobile phone while driving, Bluetooth headsets aren't a license to forget your manners and common courtesy. It's important to respect other people's personal space while you're in public. Too many people babble on their Bluetooth headsets (and mobile phones) at full register with no concern for the people around them. Don't be that person! End your call when you're around other people (especially in confined spaces) or at least keep your voice down.

Bluetooth profiles

Bluetooth isn't limited to wireless headsets. It's also about *profiles*— wireless interface specifications for communication among Bluetooth devices. A total 28 Bluetooth profiles are available, each with a different application.

The Motorola Droids support stereo Bluetooth 2.1 and the following profiles:

- **HSP (Headset Profile).** Allows Bluetooth headsets to be paired with mobile phones. Not surprisingly, this bad boy is the most popular profile of them all because it enables an entire category of wireless Bluetooth headsets to be used with your phone.

- **HFP (Hands-Free Profile).** Allows a hands-free kit in a car to communicate with mobile phones inside the vehicle. More than 170 car manufacturers, from Audi to Volvo, now build in Bluetooth at the factory. This feature allows you to pair your phone with your car so that you can hear callers through your car's stereo system; callers hear you through a microphone installed near the driver's seat.

- **A2DP (Advanced Audio Distribution Profile).** Allows you to stream music from your Droid to a pair of wireless stereo headphones over Bluetooth—great for wireless headphones at the gym!

- **AVRCP (Audio/Video Remote Control Profile).** Provides a way to control TVs and other stereo equipment, turning the Droid into a universal remote control.

- **PBAP (Phone Book Access Profile).** Allows the exchange of Phone Book Objects between devices and is typically used between the device and a Bluetooth car kit. PBAP allows the Bluetooth in your car (see the HFP item earlier in this list) to access your contacts on your Droid so that you can look up and dial a contact's phone number from your car's touchscreen.

- **OPP (Object Push Profile).** Enables you to send pictures, business cards, and appointment details to another device. You could use OPP to exchange a contact or appointment between two mobile phones, for example, or between a mobile phone and a computer.

That brings the hardware chapter to a close. Next, I want to give you a closer look at some of Android's core software applications—Phone, Contacts, and Calendar—which I do in Chapter 5.

5

Phone, Contacts, and Calendar

Whereas Chapters 1 through 4 are designed to give you some background and get you up and running quickly with your Droid, this section of the book is a little more hands-on. Now that you've got a solid foundation of knowledge, it's time to turn your attention to productivity—specifically, to three of the core apps on the Droid.

In this chapter, I focus on three apps: Phone, Contacts, and Calendar. These apps are absolutely essential to communications and productivity. I start with the basics and then show you a few tips that will improve your productivity and hone your skills.

Phone

Despite the emphasis on everything that smartphones can do, the phone is the most important component of these amazing devices. If your new smartphone doesn't work well as a *phone*—if it isn't reliable, and if it doesn't allow you to make an emergency phone call easily—it's basically useless and potentially even dangerous.

The Droid has all the features that you'd expect in a smartphone, and then some. As the Android operating system continues to evolve, it's only going to get more features. At the end of the day, though, it needs to be a solid phone. Angry Birds can't call a tow truck when your car is broken down on the side of the road.

Phone app

The Droid's Phone app (**Figure 5.1**) is very sleek and simply designed, with four tabs across the top that give you easy access to all of its core functions:

■ **Dialer.** This feature allows you to touch the screen to dial a number (although many people find it faster to dial from the Recent and Contacts tabs).

■ **Recent.** This call log displays a list of your recent inbound and outbound calls. Pressing the Menu button gives you the option to clear the log.

■ **Contacts.** The Contacts tab contains all the names and phone numbers stored on your Droid. I discuss this feature in more detail in the next major section of this chapter.

■ **Favorites.** This tab is where you store frequently dialed numbers (family, friends, the office, and so on) in one convenient location. Touching the star icon next to a contact adds it to your Favorites list.

Below the traditional 12-key dialpad is a row of three buttons: Voicemail, Call, and Voice Commands.

Figure 5.1
*The ubiquitous
Android Phone
app.*

Voicemail
Call
Voice Commands

Incoming and outgoing calls

Making a phone call couldn't get much easier. Simply follow these steps:

1. Dial a number (including the area code, if it's not in yours).

2. Touch the green Call button to initiate the phone call.

   While the phone is dialing, you see a series of call options (**Figure 5.2**):

Figure 5.2
*Several call
options are
displayed while
dialing.*

- **Add Call,** which starts a conference call (see the upcoming "Conference calls" section)

- **End Call,** which hangs up the call

- **Hide** or **Dialpad,** which conceal or bring back the dialpad (**Figure 5.3**)

Figure 5.3
Dialpad displayed during a call.

- **Bluetooth,** which enables a wireless headset

- **Mute,** which comes in handy for any number of reasons, including sparing the recipient of your call the shriek of a siren passing in the street

- **Speaker,** which places the call on speakerphone (see the next section)

3. Listen for the other party, and start talking when you hear him.

Because my daughter mastered this task at around age 1, I'm going to assume that you've got it covered.

When someone calls your Droid, her phone number is displayed on your screen. If the caller is in your contacts list, her name appears in addition to the number. To answer, touch the green Call button.

As with most other mobile phones on the market, touching the red End Call button—you guessed it—ends the phone call. No surprises there.

Speakerphone

To access the Droid's speakerphone feature, press the Menu button during any phone call to display the call-options screen (refer to Figure 5.2) and then touch Speaker. You'll hear your caller through the phone's larger speaker, and he'll hear you through the built-in microphone.

The speakerphone is excellent for long calls. It also comes in handy when someone's giving you instructions on how to upgrade your computer, for example, or when you need both hands free for delicate work or have to crawl under a desk.

note As handy as the speakerphone is, use it with discretion. Do *you* like being put on speakerphone? Most people don't, so ask for permission first. Also use it sparingly. Being underneath a car that you're trying to repair is a legitimate reason to put someone on speakerphone, but touching Speaker all the time because you're too lazy to hold the phone isn't.

Hang up and Drive

Using a speakerphone while driving is popular because it allows you to keep both hands on the wheel. Many U.S. states have passed laws making it illegal to operate a mobile phone while operating a motor vehicle, and speakerphones fall into a gray area. Driving while talking over a speakerphone technically is allowed in most states, but the phone has to be sitting on the seat or in a cup holder—*not* in your hand. As soon as you touch it to dial or hang up, you may be breaking the law.

I don't recommend using the speakerphone feature while driving because it's still a distraction. Instead, pick up a good Bluetooth headset (which I cover in Chapter 4).

Conference calls

Another powerful and somewhat underused feature of most mobile phones these days is conference calling. Conference calls are a super-handy way to shore up plans with multiple people, and they're dead simple to set up on the Droid, so there's really no excuse not to learn how to do it. Here's how:

1. When you have one person on the phone, press the Menu button to reveal the call-options screen (refer to Figure 5.2).

2. Touch Add Call, and dial the next party.

3. When the second party is on the line, press the Menu button again to reopen the call-options screen.

4. Touch Merge Calls (**Figure 5.4**).

Figure 5.4
*Merge calls from
this screen.*

Congratulations—you've made your first conference call on your Droid. I told you that it would be easy!

note There's no physical limit on the number of people you can have on a conference call on Android—just a practical limit. I think that managing more than five people on a call gets a little hard, but hey, that's me.

Call waiting

Just like your landline phone at home (if you still have one, that is), the Droid has call waiting built in. When you're on one phone call and another call comes in, you'll see a screen that looks like **Figure 5.5**.

Figure 5.5

An incoming-call screen displays whatever details you saved for the contact, including a photo.

Most mobile carriers in the United States (including Verizon Wireless) include Caller ID in their plans, and Android displays the incoming phone number if it's not blocked or private. If the caller is in your contacts database, Droid also displays that person's name and the image that you've attached to it (see "Editing contacts" later in this chapter).

If you want to take the incoming call, touch the large Answer button to put the current call on hold and answer the new one. If you don't want to interrupt your current call, you can decline the incoming one by touching the large Ignore button. When you do, the Droid transfers the new call to voicemail.

Voicemail

One consequence of the digital age is the proliferation of voicemail. Despite what the phone carriers tell you, however, it's unrealistic to expect to reach someone on her mobile phone any time, anywhere. As much as you may not want to believe it, people have families, jobs, and lives to deal with, and taking your phone call isn't always at the top of the list.

On one hand, voicemail can be frustrating. On the other hand, when it's combined with Caller ID, voicemail may be the single greatest privacy tool in the world. How many times has it saved you from taking a phone call at an inopportune time? You probably couldn't count them.

If you miss a call on your Droid, a little status-bar alert tells you so. You can either pull down the status bar to reveal a larger notification with more information (see Chapter 3 for details on notifications), as in **Figure 5.6**, or you can get the same information by launching the Phone app and then touching the Recent tab at the top of the screen (refer to Figure 5.1 earlier in this chapter).

Figure 5.6
Missed-call information.

When you receive a voicemail message, another status-bar alert pops up. As with missed calls, pulling down the status bar gives you more information about the message, including the Caller ID information and the time the call was received. Unfortunately, if you've missed more than one call, you lose this information and see only the number of calls you've missed.

Touching the voicemail notification icon in the status bar is the fastest way to dial your voicemail. To retrieve a message, touch the status bar and slide it down; then touch the Missed Calls alert.

note   The key commands for saving and deleting voicemail vary from carrier to carrier, so I'm not going to cover them in this book.

tip   It's best to listen to the automated instructions all the way to the end when you first set up voicemail. This recording provides copious details on the carrier's voicemail system, and it's good to take the time to learn all the options. Settle into a comfy chair and kick up your feet while you set up voicemail on your Droid. Soon, the commands will become familiar, and before too long, they'll be second nature.

Call forwarding

Call forwarding isn't nearly as sexy as some of the other features, but it's quite handy nonetheless. Suppose that you're taking a quick trip with your spouse, and you don't want to carry two phones. You can simply forward one phone's calls to the other. Call forwarding becomes essential when you've lost or misplaced a phone: Just forward your calls to another phone, and you're back in business (sort of). When your calls are forwarded, any new calls that come to the lost phone are forwarded to the other phone. Call forwarding can be your best friend when you lose your phone.

The Droid's Call Settings screen (**Figure 5.7** on the next page) allows you to enable automatic retry (handy for those mind-numbing repeat calls to Ticketmaster), TTY, hearing-aid compatibility, and enhanced voice privacy.

Figure 5.7
The Droid's Call Settings screen has lots of options.

Because Android 2.2 (Froyo) doesn't provide a call-forwarding option, for whatever reason, you'll have to enable it the old-fashioned way: Dial *72 followed by the ten-digit number that you want to forward your phone to, and touch the green phone icon to dial. When you want to disable call forwarding, dial *73 and touch the dial icon. The problem with this method is that you get no confirmation that call forwarding is set, and no indicator is displayed in the status bar to remind you that it's on.

tip If your Droid is lost or stolen, you can forward its calls to another phone by calling Verizon Wireless customer support at (800) 922-0204. If your account is set up for online access, you can also manage your call-forwarding settings at www.myverizon.com.

The good news is that Google is continually updating the Android operating system, and call forwarding has been spotted on other Android phones. With any luck, the Droid will get a dedicated call-forwarding option in a future release of Android.

Forward with Care

Keep in mind a few caveats before enabling call forwarding:

- The Droid must be powered up to forward calls. If its battery runs out, calls will no longer be forwarded.

- Airtime (minutes) applies to forwarded and transferred calls, even if you send the call to a landline (aka wireline) telephone.

- If you forward calls from your Droid to another mobile, *both* phones are using airtime.

- Don't forward calls to long-distance numbers if your plan doesn't include them. When you forward calls to numbers outside your local calling area, you're responsible for any toll, long-distance, and airtime charges incurred.

Contacts

Although I say earlier in this chapter that the phone is the Droid's most important feature, the Contacts app actually ties it for first place. Without your contacts, how would you remember a person's phone number, email address, or Twitter handle?

Contacts play a critical role on a mobile phone because they're your link to the outside world. They allow you to communicate with everyone who's important to you, which is a lot of people. Businesspeople would argue that contacts are *everything* because they're sources of revenue.

People seem to change phone numbers, email addresses, and street addresses more frequently than ever these days, making it important to be vigilant about keeping your contact data current—if you want to actually reach anyone, that is. It's a never-ending task, which may be why Americans spend billions of dollars each year on contact management or customer relationship management software.

If you have a Droid, however, you can save that money, because your device includes excellent data synchronization software. Google has simplified the process tremendously by storing everything on the cloud, making it easier to keep your ever-expanding contacts current. The process requires a little training and discipline, but storing your contact data on the cloud has two big benefits:

* You can access it anywhere that you can get an Internet connection.

* It's virtually impossible to lose your data (unlike your phone, which you have a 50 percent chance of losing).

Managing contacts on the phone

You have two main ways to manage contacts on the Droid:

* Launch the Phone app, and touch the Contacts tab.

* Launch the Contacts app from the app tray by touching its icon (refer to Chapter 3).

Either way, you see your list of contacts, which you can add to or edit as I describe in the following sections.

When you're viewing the Contacts list, pressing the Menu button displays two options at the bottom of the screen (**Figure 5.8**):

* **Search.** This option is pretty self-explanatory. Touch it to search your contacts.

* **Speed Dial Setup.** This option allows you to set up ten contacts that you can dial instantly by long-pressing one of the numbers in the Dialer tab.

Figure 5.8
The Contacts tab has two options.

Adding contacts

To add a new contact, follow these steps:

1. Launch the Phone app.

2. Touch the phone number.

3. Touch Dialer > Menu > Add to Contacts.

4. Touch either New or Existing.

    The Edit Contact screen opens (**Figure 5.9**).

Figure 5.9
Create a contact easily by entering some contact data and touching Save.

5. Fill in the appropriate details.

6. Optionally, you can scroll down to touch the Additional Info button at the bottom of the screen (not visible in Figure 5.9) and enter even more data.

   More data is always better than less, so if you have the time, enter as much contact data as possible.

7. Touch the Save button when you're finished.

Contacts entered on the Droid are automagically synced to the Google cloud in the background—an amazingly useful and powerful feature.

Editing contacts

To edit or delete a contact, follow these steps:

1. Touch Phone > Contacts to display your list of contacts.

2. Search or use the scroll tab on the right side of the screen to find the contact you want.

3. Touch the contact's name to display its detail view (**Figure 5.10**).

Figure 5.10
A contact's detail view.

4. Press the Menu button; then touch the resulting Edit button to open the Edit Contact screen (**Figure 5.11**).

Figure 5.11
The Edit Contact screen for an existing contact.

5. Edit any of the fields for that contact.

6. Touch the Save button when you're finished.

7. If you want to delete a contact, just press Menu > Delete Contact in any contact-editing screen.

If you want to get fancy, you can add photos of your contacts to their contact information by touching the picture icon in the top-left corner of the Edit Contact screen (as I've done with the skiers in Figure 5.11). Remember to touch Save when you're finished. Then, whenever you call a contact or a contact calls you, your Droid will display that person's picture. This feature is a nice personal touch but can take some time to set up, especially if you have a lot of contacts.

tip The contact screen for Heavenly Ski Resort (refer to Figure 5.10) is a great example of a clean, well-populated screen. Having complete contact data like this example makes interacting with your contacts infinitely easier and faster, and it's well worth your investment in time.

Your All-Star Contacts

Although you may have hundreds—or even thousands—of contacts stored on your phone, odds are that you probably call about a dozen of them 80 percent of the time. To make it easy to find the friends and family members whom you call all the time, make them favorites. Think of the process as creating bookmarks or shortcuts for those contacts.

To create a favorite, just touch the star in the top-right corner of the contact screen (refer to Figure 5.10). This places the contact in the Phone app's Favorites tab (refer to Figure 5.1 at the start of this chapter) so that it's easy to find and redial in the future.

You can star a contact in that person's Edit Contact screen on the Web as well as in the Droid interface. Just go to www.google.com/contacts, click a contact, and then click the Edit button near the top of the screen.

Managing contacts with Google Contacts

Real-time, online data synchronization isn't a trivial task. Many companies have failed miserably at it by underestimating what's involved and how complicated it really is. Someone once summed up the situation by saying "Sync is hard."

But not Google. The Droid synchronizes your data—automatically and in the background—with Google Contacts (www.google.com/contacts), Calendars (www.google.com/calendars), and Gmail (www.gmail.com).

Sync is a very powerful feature, and Google got it right with Android, providing it as a free service. How you use Google Contacts depends on whether you're starting from scratch or already using it. I discuss both approaches in the following sections.

Starting contacts from scratch

If you're new to Google, perhaps creating a new Google account just for your Droid, you should take a bit of time to set up your contacts. As I mention earlier in this chapter, contacts are integral to your phone, and having them organized and up to date is essential to having a good Droid experience.

Importing contacts

You can import any contacts in CSV (comma-separated values) file format. The easiest way is to use the import tool in Google Contacts. Just follow these steps on your computer:

1. Log in to Google Contacts (www.google.com/contacts) from any Web browser.

2. Click the Import link in the top-right corner of the screen to open the My Contacts window (**Figure 5.12**).

Figure 5.12

Many people find it easier to add and import contacts on a desktop computer, using a real keyboard.

3. Select the contact file you want to use.

4. Click Import.

If you're using Windows, you can import data from Microsoft Outlook, Outlook Express, Yahoo Mail, Hotmail, Eudora, and some other apps. Just export the contact data to a CSV file and then import that file into Google Contacts.

If you're using Address Book on a Mac, you have several ways to import contacts into Google:

■ The simplest method is to choose Address Book > Preferences > Accounts, check the Synchronize with Google check box, and then click the Google button. You'll be prompted to log in with your Google account, and Address Book will sync in the background.

■ A free utility for the Mac called A to G (www.macupdate.com/info. php/id/26427/a-to-g) exports a tidy CSV file to your desktop; this file imports easily into Google Contacts. The A to G utility is good for one-way migration to Google but doesn't offer syncing.

■ An app called Spanning Sync (www.spanningsync.com; $25 for one year or $65 for a permanent license) allows Mac users to synchronize Address Book and iCal with Google Contacts and Calendars. The app may seem to be a little expensive, but it's worth the cost because it syncs bidirectionally (from Mac to Google, and vice versa) in the background.

Entering contacts manually

If you don't have a software app that Google Contacts can import contacts from, you can enter contacts directly by clicking the blue icon in the top-left corner of the Google Contacts window—the one showing one person next to a plus sign (refer to Figure 5.12 in the preceding section). Then just populate the fields, save your work, and move to the next contact.

note You can add multiple phone numbers and email, street, and instant-messaging (IM) addresses by clicking the blue Add link next to each field name. You can also add custom fields for notes and other things by clicking More Information at the bottom of the window.

tip You can sync directly from Apple's Address Book by choosing Preferences > Accounts (Figure 5.13). If you want to perform a one-time import from Address Book, use the freeware utility A to G (which I discuss in the preceding section).

Figure 5.13
The preferences screen of Apple's Address Book application.

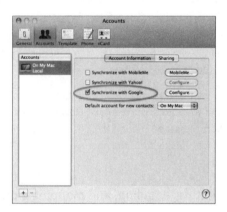

Already using Google Contacts

If you're already using Gmail or Google Contacts as your primary contact manager, you're way ahead of the game. Your contacts already live on the cloud and are ready to go; in fact, they've probably downloaded to your Droid already. Take a gander at the Contacts screen in the Phone app (refer to "Managing contacts on the phone" earlier in this chapter). If you see contacts that you didn't add manually, you're in business. How easy was that?

Troubleshooting contacts

If you're not seeing your Google Contacts entries on your Droid, here are a few things to check:

- Did you sign in on your phone under the same account that you use for Google Contacts? Getting the account sign-on right is imperative. If you have more than one Google account, you may find it easy to mix up those accounts.

- Are you in an area that has a solid data connection? Can you surf Web pages? If not, the problem is with your Internet connection.

- If you set up your phone recently (as in hours ago), the contacts may not have fully synced from the cloud to your phone yet. Patience, Jedi, patience. Give it an hour or two.

After you've verified that your Google Contacts are synced between the cloud and your Droid, you're all set! Now you can call, email, IM, text (via Short Message Service [SMS]), or even map the address of any of your contacts directly from the phone—all of which I discuss in the next section.

Dialing, texting, emailing, and mapping a contact

Any time you're viewing contacts, you can communicate with that particular person or business in a couple of ways, right from the contact list:

- If you long-press a contact's photo, a little bar pops up, displaying contact options (**Figure 5.14**). Touch the appropriate option to call, email, text, or map that contact.

- To the right of each piece of data in the contact's detail screen (refer to Figure 5.10 earlier in this chapter) is an icon representing the contact's phone number, email address, and so on. As you've probably guessed, touching that icon calls, messages, emails, or maps the contact that you're viewing. This feature is incredibly useful and centralizes all the ways to communicate with that contact.

Figure 5.14
Long-pressing a contact's photo reveals the Quick Contact bar.

Touch to view contact.

Touch to launch VZ Navigator.

Touch to call.

Touch to email.

Touch to open the Browser app.

Heavenly Ski Resort...

Calendar

There's no question that the phone and Contacts features are integral parts of your mobile-phone experience. I close the chapter with the third biggie: Calendar.

Calendar is very feature-rich and frankly tough to beat, especially for the price. Google synchronizes its online calendars directly to Android phones over the air and completely free of charge. Many of the principles that I outline for Contacts earlier in this chapter apply to the Calendar app on the Droid; also, the two apps are linked in many ways. (If you jumped directly to this section, I recommend that you read the "Contacts" section before proceeding.)

The concept is simple: You can manage calendar events on the Droid itself or on the Web, depending on what suits you. Most people find it easier to enter and manage their calendars on a desktop computer because of the familiar keyboard and large screen. Droid syncing is bidirectional, so you can edit in either place, or both, and Google keeps both calendars in sync.

As with Google Contacts, the way you use Google Calendar depends on whether you're starting from scratch or already using it. I cover both methods in the next two sections.

Starting a calendar from scratch

If you're new to Google or have just created a new Google account for use with your Droid, you should take some time to set up your calendars. Like the phone and contacts, calendars are integral to the Droid experience, and having them organized will make you more productive.

Entering calendar events manually

The easiest way to enter calendar events is via the Web interface. Follow these steps on your computer:

1. Log in to Google Calendar (www.google.com/calendar).

2. Click the Create Event link in the top-left corner of the screen (**Figure 5.15**).

Figure 5.15

Events are easy to create in the Google Calendar Web interface.

3. Fill in the fields, and set the options.

   For details, see "Working with events and reminders" later in this chapter.

4. Click Save.

Importing calendar events

If you already maintain a calendar in iCal or Microsoft Outlook, you can import it into Google Calendar with the handy online import tool (www. google.com/calendar). The only catch is that event information must be in iCal or CSV (Outlook) format. If you're using a calendar program that doesn't export to one of those formats, you need to export the calendar data to a format that Google Calendar can read.

To import calendar data into Google Calendar from a desktop computer, choose Add > Import Calendar; click the Add link in the Other Calendars section (bottom-left corner) to open the Calendar Settings screen (**Figure 5.16**); and then browse to the file that you exported from your other calendar app.

Figure 5.16
Import calendar data from this screen.

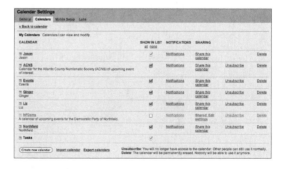

If you're new to Google Calendar, now would be a good time to famil-iarize yourself with the full version on your desktop computer at your own pace. The balance of this chapter focuses primarily on calendars on the Droid.

Already using Google Calendar

If you're already using Google Calendar, pat yourself on the back, put your feet up, and maybe even take an afternoon nap. Your calendar events are already on the cloud and may already be synced to your Droid!

Launch the Calendar app on the Droid. If it looks like **Figure 5.17**, you're in business. Your calendar is already synced. If it's blank, with no color bar on the right edge of each date, either you have a light month planned or your calendar isn't synced (see "Troubleshooting contacts" earlier in this chapter; those tips also apply to calendars).

Figure 5.17
The Calendar app on the Droid.

After you've verified that your Google Calendar data is synced between the cloud and your Droid, you're ready to roll. You can view your calendars, create events, and receive reminders.

Viewing a calendar

People most commonly use Google Calendar simply to view a calendar. About 90 percent of the calendaring I do on my phone is checking what's coming up today, this week, and this month. Usually, when a friend asks something like "Do you want to see Furthur on March 22"?, I'll whip out my phone, fire up Calendar, and zoom to that date.

Scroll between months by swiping your finger up and down the screen.

Pressing the Menu button while you're in the Calendar app (conveniently located in the app tray; refer to Chapter 3) gives you options to view a day, week, or month at a time (**Figure 5.18**). Month view can get kind of cramped on the Droid's small screen, but luckily, touching a day switches you to day view, where you can read the details about events.

Figure 5.18
The Calendar in month view with menu options exposed.

Using other calendars

Your calendar is very important because it allows you to make meetings and your kid's gymnastics class on time—but that's only the beginning. Google also allows you to create and maintain multiple calendars for things like clubs, groups, and sports leagues that you're involved in. One amazingly useful feature lets you view your significant other's calendar. Just have him or her set up a Google calendar and then click Add a Friend's Calendar in the Other Calendars section (refer to Figure 5.15 earlier in this chapter).

Also, you can sign up for an assortment of public calendars by choosing Add > Browse Interesting Calendars (**Figure 5.19** on the next page).

Calendars for everything from U.S. to international holidays and fun things like phases of the moon are accessible from the Google Calendar Web interface.

Figure 5.19
Some of the many interesting (and free!) Google calendars available.

> **tip** I recommend setting up separate calendars for your work and personal events so that your vet appointments and sales meetings don't mix. Don't worry, though; you can still overlay all your calendars on one master calendar and view everything at the same time. Keeping separate calendars is best because it allows you to toggle the work calendar off while you're away on vacation and share only personal events with your family members (who couldn't care less about your next daily status meeting, thankyouverymuch!).

You can control which calendars you see on the Droid by pressing the Menu button and then touching More > Calendars. The Calendars screen (**Figure 5.20**) allows you to adjust how your calendars behave, and I usually keep mine set to Synced, Visible. Touch that creepy-looking arrows-and-eye icon to the right of each calendar to toggle its settings.

Figure 5.20
My Calendars allows you to select which calendars to view.

You can add and delete calendars by pressing the Menu button while you're in the My Calendars screen. You'll see two buttons at the bottom of the screen for—what else?—adding and removing calendars. Didn't I tell you that this was going to be easy?

Working with events and reminders

When a friend asks whether you're available on a certain day, and you discover that you are by checking your calendar, it's best to create a new event right there on the spot. Sure, it's easy to say that you'll remember the event and put it in your calendar later, but if you're like me, doing that is virtually impossible. If I don't enter an event in my calendar right away, it usually doesn't happen. Taking time to create a new event the minute that it's confirmed will pay off down the road.

You have two primary ways to create events (or appointments, or meetings) on the Droid:

- Touch Calendar > Menu > New Event.
- Long-press a specific day and time in any of the calendar views (day, week, or month).

Either method brings up the Edit Event screen (**Figure 5.21**). Just complete a few of the whos and whats about the event, and touch the Save button (not visible in the figure). The new event immediately appears on your Droid's calendar and synchronizes with the desktop version of Google Calendar within a few minutes.

Figure 5.21
The Edit Event screen allows you to view and edit details.

Reminders are important aspects of the whole event-creation process and, therefore, worth reviewing. When you add a new event, by default the phone is set to give you a lowly 10-minute reminder, which isn't enough time to make it to the dry cleaner's down the street, let alone to catch a flight. You can set reminders any time you create or edit a calendar event (on the phone or on the Web) as far as a week out, but I usually choose a 2-hour reminder for local events, which allows me enough time for preparation and travel.

Reminder icons appear in the status bar and can be expanded to show more detail.

What's the Agenda?

If the day, week, and month views aren't your cup of tea, you're not alone. The month and week views can get cluttered and hard to read pretty quickly if you have more than three events per day (not as hard as it sounds). Fear not, fair reader! Google has a solution for that problem too: the Agenda (**Figure 5.22**).

Figure 5.22

The Agenda list is the most useful Calendar view.

The Agenda is essentially a list of all your upcoming events from all synced calendars, displayed in a nice clean interface. It shows the name of the event, the date(s), location, alarm, URL, repeating status (the circling-arrows icon), and the calendar color. Touch an event in any view to view and edit the event details (**Figure 5.23**).

Figure 5.23

The Agenda's View Event screen.

The Agenda is by far the easiest calendar view to read and use, which is probably why it's the first option you see when you press the Menu button in the Calendar app. You'll use it a lot. I rarely look at the other calendar views because it's so much quicker to flick and scroll through the Agenda.

Caveat Calendar

Like many other things in life, Google Calendar does have a couple of limitations:

- As with most Google apps, I find it quicker to do any substantial editing in the full version of the app on a desktop computer. For entering anything more than a few words, I'm much faster at typing on my full desktop keyboard than on any mobile device's keyboard, and nothing beats a big screen, especially for viewing a busy month in Google Calendar.

- At this writing, several features of the desktop version of Google Calendar haven't made it to the Android edition: sending invitations, creating calendars, sharing calendars, and adding a public calendar.

I wouldn't worry too much about these limitations, though. All the important features are in the Android edition now, and a lot of talented coders at Google headquarters are on the case. I wouldn't be surprised if Google Calendar could paint your house by the time you read this book.

That wraps up Droid's three core apps: Phone, Contacts, and Calendar. As with anything, you'll get more proficient with use, so it's important to embrace these core apps and put them to work for you. Time invested in them now will pay off in more free time in the future—or at least in fewer missed meetings.

In Chapter 6, I take a look at three other critical pieces of the Droid software: email, messaging, and Web browsing.

6

Email, Messaging, and Web

Now that I've given you a look at three fundamental Droid apps (Phone, Contacts, and Calendar), it's time to turn your attention to three critical communication apps: Email, Messaging, and Web browsing.

Many people purchase a Droid specifically for its capability to send and receive email. Email is one of the defining features of a smartphone, and if your Droid has a QWERTY keyboard (like the Droid 2 and Droid Pro), you'll be tapping out emails as fast as you can on your desktop computer.

> **note** A lot of development resources are being devoted to voice recognition, too, so look for a proliferation of applications that will accept and transcribe your voice in the not-too-distant future.

In this chapter, I jump-start your knowledge of Android's mail and messaging applications, take a close look at the practical use of these applications, and provide some tips and tricks for good measure. I round out the chapter with a look at the Droid's excellent Web browser—arguably the most powerful app on any smartphone.

Email

The Droid allows you to take your email with you wherever you go, making it even more convenient than a desktop or even a notebook computer. Droid supports several types of email: corporate (Microsoft Exchange 2003 and 2007), Gmail, IMAP, POP3 with full support for attachments, and Microsoft Office and Adobe PDF documents.

The Droid comes with two email applications, Email and Gmail (**Figure 6.1**)—and actually comes with three if you count the Web browser. The first is a universal email client that you can use to access any email account based on POP3 or IMAP, and the second is Google's popular Web-based email service, which many users regard as being the best.

Figure 6.1
Android's Email and Gmail applications allow you to stay connected almost anywhere.

Email   Gmail

note POP3 (Post Office Protocol, Version 3) and IMAP (Internet Message Access Protocol) are the dominant email protocols.

tip Corporate email allows clients of Exchange 2003 or 2007 servers to synchronize email, contacts, and calendars over the Droid's wireless Internet connection. Contact your company's information technology (IT) department for the settings for your Exchange server.

Using Gmail

Google began offering Webmail service under the Gmail moniker publicly in 2007, although it was available as a private beta application as early as 2004. The service, officially named Google Mail, has more than 146 million monthly users, largely because of its simple yet powerful interface and high storage capacity (currently, more than 7 GB per account). It's also desirable for people who receive large attachments, because a Gmail account will accept attachments as large as 25 MB—more than double the capacity of its competitors.

In addition to being intuitive enough for my 80-year-old mother-in-law to use, Gmail is loaded with features such as a powerful search utility (no surprise there!). It also provides a threaded view called *conversations* that allows you to see all messages with the same subject in one convenient screen without having to hunt through your inbox for previous messages on the same topic.

The main Gmail view is the inbox, which lists all your messages in reverse chronological order (**Figure 6.2**).

Figure 6.2

The Gmail app's inbox.

The most powerful feature of Gmail in Android shows new messages in your inbox as they arrive without your having to refresh the inbox or check your email. This feature, called *push*, means that your Gmail inbox is up to date at all times.

Launching the app

Because Gmail is tied to the Google account that you set up earlier (refer to Chapter 2), you don't have anything to configure. Just launch the application by touching its shortcut, and you'll be greeted by your inbox.

As you accumulate email in your account, you'll see your most recent email at the top of the main screen (your inbox). To see older emails, just drag your finger from the bottom to the top of the screen—a technique called *flicking*.

Reading an email is as simple as touching it in the inbox. When you do, you see the subject line, sender, and date, followed by the message itself.

tip **Android 2.0's universal inbox allows you to view the latest email from all your accounts in one simple interface, which sure beats switching among multiple email accounts—a process that takes multiple touches.**

Because Gmail can display HTML messages, emails are rendered beautifully on the Droid via *antialiasing,* a technology that generates smooth round edges and easy-to-read, eye-pleasing text.

Viewing inbox options

Pressing the Menu button while you're viewing the inbox gives you access to the six options shown at the bottom of **Figure 6.3**.

Figure 6.3
To access Gmail options, press the Menu button while you're viewing the inbox.

You'll see these options:

- **Refresh.** For the truly impatient, this option forces the inbox to refresh (although refreshing technically isn't required, thanks to Gmail's push feature).

- **Compose.** Touch this option to write a new email.

- **Accounts.** Touch this option to switch among multiple accounts or to add a new account.

- **Go to Labels.** This option, which is another way to filter your email, displays only email with a given label (see "Managing mail" later in this chapter).

- **Search.** This option allows you to search your email for a keyword or phrase.

- **More.** The Settings option gives you access to further options in the General Settings screen (**Figure 6.4** on the next page):

Figure 6.4

Gmail's general settings allow you to do things like add a signature and receive a status-bar notification when you get new email.

- **Priority Inbox.** This setting automatically identifies important email and separates it from everything else.

- **Signature.** The Signature setting allows you to add a custom footer to messages that you compose. Usually, a signature contains contact information.

- **Confirm Actions.** This setting displays a confirmation dialog box when you mark an email for deletion (see "Managing mail" later in this chapter).

- **Reply All.** This setting makes Reply All the default when you respond to email messages. (I recommend leaving this option unchecked so that you don't accidentally respond to a group when you intended to reply only to the sender.)

- **Auto-Advance.** This setting lets you select which screen is shown after you archive or delete a conversation.

- **Message Text Size.** Choose among Tiny, Small, Normal, Large, and Huge.

- **Batch Operations.** This setting allows you to apply labels to multiple email conversations.

Managing mail

Here's a little trick that saves me a lot of time: Long-press a message in the inbox view to access email options without having to open the message. These options are

- **Read.** Allows you to read the message as though you'd touched it normally. (I know—duh!)

- **Archive.** Moves messages out of your inbox, letting you tidy up your inbox without deleting anything.

- **Mute.** Keeps your inbox free of unwanted threads. Here's how: When you *mute* a message, follow-up emails to the conversation bypass the inbox. If you're being copied on a thread that doesn't involve you (or that you'd like to ignore), touch Mute.

- **Mark Unread.** Allows you to mark a message as unread while reading it. This setting is handy for remembering that you need to come back to an email.

- **Delete.** Removes a message or conversation from Gmail—eventually. *Delete* is actually a misnomer here. When you delete an email in Android, it's actually stashed in the Trash folder on the Droid for 30 days; *then* it's deleted.

> **tip** Deleting emails can clear out some of your storage space, but with Gmail's free storage, it's best to keep all your emails. If you just want to get an email out of your face, I recommend using the Archive option instead.

- **Add/Remove Star.** Adds a star next to certain messages or conversations to give them special status, or removes said star. Starred items remain visible when you return to a conversation.

- **Change Labels.** Changes the label attached to a particular email. Think of labels as being folders with a bonus: You can add more than one label to an email. In your inbox, press the Menu button and then touch Go to Labels (see the preceding section) to narrow your email view.

- **Report Spam.** Allows you to report a message as spam without opening it. When you do, the offending pork product is removed from your inbox, and you help Google prevent more like it from arriving.

Using the Email app

Not everyone chooses Gmail as his or her email provider, because most people had another email account before Gmail came along. To serve non-Gmail users, Google includes a more generic Email application on the Droid that lets you access an unlimited number of POP3 and/or IMAP accounts.

Setting up the Email app on the Droid couldn't be easier, thanks to a convenient wizard that walks you through the process the first time you launch the application.

note Before you embark on this little journey, you have to provide some information, such as your password, incoming and outgoing email servers, and any special ports. It's best to assemble this information before you start.

Setting up your account

To set up your account by using the Email application's setup wizard, follow these steps:

1. Enter your email address and password (**Figure 6.5**); then touch Next.

   If you enter an address from a popular Webmail service such as Yahoo or Hotmail, the wizard automatically completes most of the settings for you—a nice feature.

Figure 6.5
*The Email app's
setup wizard
first asks for
your address and
password.*

tip   **If you're an expert, you can dispense with the wizard and enter your
settings in four concise screens by clearing the Automatically
Configure Account check box.**

2. In the next screen, enter your general settings (**Figure 6.6**); then
   touch OK.

Figure 6.6
*The General
Settings screen.*

Account Name is anything that you want to name the account; Real Name is what appears as the From address on email that you send; and Email Address is, of course, your email address.

3. In the next screen, enter your incoming server settings, including your user name, password, server, port, and security type (**Figure 6.7**); then touch OK.

Figure 6.7
Enter your incoming server settings here.

The drop-down menu at the top of the screen is typically set to IMAP or POP3; check with your Internet service provider (ISP) or the IT folks if you don't know which to choose. The Server and Port settings are also provided by your ISP. Your user name is usually the first part of your email address, but some ISPs require you to enter your complete address as your user name. Password is self-explanatory.

tip Instead of waiting on hold with technical support to get your email settings, try checking the incoming and outgoing account information in your desktop computer's email application. You can glean most of the necessary settings there, although your password will be bulleted out. If you can't remember your password, you may have to make that call.

4. Enter your outgoing server settings in the next screen (**Figure 6.8**); then touch OK.

Figure 6.8
Enter your outgoing server settings here.

Get your SMTP Server and Port settings from your ISP or the IT crew. Then enter the same user name and password that you entered in the Incoming Server screen (refer to step 3). If you're not sure whether your server uses secure connections (also called Secure Sockets Layer [SSL]), check both boxes at the bottom of this screen.

note Thanks to the scourge of spam, ISPs have been forced to add security to their outgoing mail servers. The user name and password you enter here usually are the same ones that you use for your email account, but definitely check with your ISP if you're not sure.

5. Complete the Other Settings screen (**Figure 6.9**) if necessary.

Figure 6.9
*The Other
Settings screen is
pretty barren.*

The Number of Messages to Sync setting allows you to set the
number of emails that you want to sync from the server at the same
time. The default is 25, and I leave it set at that on my Droid.

6. Touch OK one final time, and you're home free (**Figure 6.10**).

Figure 6.10
*If all went well,
you'll see the
Success! screen,
and what could
be better than
that?*

7. Touch the Done button in the Success! screen.

You see your inbox (**Figure 6.11**), with your most recent emails (sender's address, subject line, and date) listed at the top of the screen.

Figure 6.11
The Email app's inbox.

> **tip** Long-pressing an email in the inbox reveals a drop-down box that allows you to open, delete, forward, reply all, reply, or mark as unread in one quick step.

Reading, replying, and composing

Assuming that you didn't jump right to this section from the table of contents, you can probably guess how to do most of the things associated with email. Reading, replying to, and composing emails are extremely intuitive tasks on the Droid, and most functions are only a screen touch away.

You handle pretty much everything else by pressing the Menu button and then touching the desired option (refer to Figure 6.3 earlier in this chapter). Rather than repeat all that information here (this book is a *Pocket Guide,* after all!), I refer you to the "Viewing inbox options" and "Managing mail" sections of the Gmail topic earlier in this chapter.

There you have it. Your email is popping!

Messaging

Text messaging is the new email, at least when it comes to mobile phones. The extreme convenience of text messaging has contributed to its meteoric rise in popularity over the past decade. It's used by approximately 75 percent of mobile-phone subscribers, translating into 2.4 billion active users and 15 billion messages sent each year. Whew!

Sending messages via Short Message Service (SMS), or just *texting,* is ideal for those times when you want to convey a message that's not long enough for an email or important enough to justify a phone call. It's also handy for times when you don't want to disrupt the recipient with a phone call but can't wait for him to check his email.

Because they're limited to 160 characters (about 25 words, give or take), text messages force you to summarize what you could probably talk about for 20 minutes on the phone or ramble on about for 11 paragraphs in an email. For many people, this very brevity makes texting so power-ful—and it doesn't hurt that most phones (including the Droid) notify you when you have an SMS message via an in-your-face alert.

Like all good technologies, SMS got an upgrade in 2002 to Multimedia Messaging Service (MMS), which allows users to send longer messages and include images, audio, video, and rich text. It's most popular for send-ing photos from camera-equipped phones.

The Droid comes with both SMS and MMS in one convenient application called Messaging. In the following sections, I go over some of the features of both types of messaging, so stretch those thumbs; they're about to get a workout.

note If you get bitten by the texting bug, you need to invest in an unlimited text package. It's easy to exceed the number of text messages included in your plan (if you get any, that is), and at 20 cents per outgoing or incoming message, overages can add up quickly. If you have teenage children, just buck up for the unlimited plan, as you'll probably be texting them when dinner is ready.

Short Message Service

The beauty of SMS is its simplicity—no complicated configuration, no difficult settings, and frankly not much to learn. You start using it by launching the Messaging application (with a simple touch of its shortcut in the home screen). When the app loads, you see the Messaging inbox, displaying the messages you've received in reverse chronological order (**Figure 6.12**).

Figure 6.12

The messaging inbox isn't much different from the email inbox— just a little spiffier, thanks to the picture thumbnails.

The first 35 characters of received messages are visible in the inbox view, along with the sender, time, and date. If the sender is in your contact list (see Chapter 5 for more on contacts), you'll see her proper name displayed; if not, you see just her mobile-phone number. Messages sent from your carrier often display partial numbers and don't accept replies. Fortunately, carriers don't charge for these messages.

The quickest way to compose a message is to touch the first line of the Messaging inbox, labeled New Text Message. Another way is to press the Menu button, touch the Compose icon, enter a contact's name (or phone number) in the To field, write a message, and then touch the Send button.

When you receive a text or multimedia message, a notification icon in the status bar tells you so. Slide the status bar down and touch the message to go directly to the Messaging app's detail view (**Figure 6.13**), where you can view the entire conversation (if any) and reply to the sender. Touching any message in the inbox also takes you to detail view.

Figure 6.13

The messaging detail view displays the sender's thumbnail image plus any inline MMS objects, like the photo in this thread.

To set SMS options, press the Menu button and then touch Settings. The
Settings screen (**Figure 6.14**) contains several options that are pretty self-
explanatory, thanks to the help text below each option.

Figure 6.14

*The Messaging
app's Settings
screen lists a
variety of useful
options.*

> **tip** The coolest feature of SMS and MMS messages is the Delivery Reports
> option. When you enable this option, the Droid sends you a message
> to confirm that your outgoing message reached its destination—similar to
> a return receipt from the post office. Unfortunately, this feature isn't a perfect
> science, so don't rely on it to be 100 percent accurate.

Multimedia Messaging Service

Multimedia Messaging Service (MMS) is the next generation of SMS.
In addition to sending a vanilla text message, you can attach images,
audio, video, and rich text, so comparing MMS with SMS is like comparing
a banana split with a vanilla cone. A better analogy would be comparing
SMS and MMS with plain text and HTML emails.

Although MMS is super-useful for sending photos from camera-equipped
phones (like all Droids), it can also be annoying when you go off the deep
end and send a birthday card that includes an animated singing frog.

As with most things in life, discretion is the better part of valor when it comes to MMS.

To send an MMS, touch New Text Message at the top of the Messaging inbox (refer to Figure 6.12 earlier in this chapter), or touch Menu > Compose. Add a recipient and some text; then touch Menu > Attach. The resulting screen (**Figure 6.15**) allows you to attach pictures, audio, video, and slideshows.

Figure 6.15
MMS trumps SMS with its support of attachments. It also allows you to send a picture to a friend instantly.

note Before you go hog-wild sending all kinds of fancy media attachments, make sure that your recipient can accept MMS messages. If he can't, he'll get a strange message asking him to log in to a Web page to retrieve it. If you're not certain that your recipient has an MMS-capable phone, send an SMS message instead.

Twitter: The New Black?

If texting is the new email, Twitter is arguably the new instant messaging (IM). I haven't used IM since switching almost exclusively to Twitter in early 2007—but that's a story for another chapter, my friend! For more Twitter fun, download the free Twitter app, which I cover in Chapter 9.

Web Browsing

By this point in the book, I hope that I don't have to explain the power of the Web. Because you've invested in a Droid (or are considering investing in one), you're probably a pretty Web-savvy person. Because my cats are fairly proficient at using the Web (hey, maybe that's where those credit-card offers are coming from!), I'd like to assume that you are too.

That said, the World Wide Web gives you access to more information than kings and other rulers had as little as 100 years ago. The Web is a much faster way to get information, too. Rather than having to dispatch a legion of serfs across land and sea to gather information, you can simply type a few keywords in Google, and boom!: Thousands of results (or even millions) are at your disposal. Results are returned in milliseconds, rather than days/weeks/months or even years. What did we do before Google?

In all seriousness, the importance, utility, and convenience of the Web are irrefutable. The Web allows you to research a book (ahem!); get prices, reviews, and dealer costs for just about anything; conduct online banking; attend meetings; and buy and sell all kinds of items. On the Droid, you start from the home screen by touching the Browser shortcut.

Mobile browsers

Although expectations can be high, it's important to understand that mobile Web browsers aren't perfect. You're limited to a small screen and keyboard, and you have less memory and storage. Otherwise, mobile-phone browsers operate pretty much like the browsers on desktop computers. You can zoom in, zoom out, and move inside a Web page.

tip **The first smartphone to come with support for Adobe Flash was the HTC Hero, released June 24, 2009. Now pretty much every new Droid includes Flash Player.**

Odds are that you've used a browser before, so I won't go into detail on the basics of a Web address and the like. Instead, I focus on how a mobile browser differs from a desktop Web browser.

First, though, some technical background is in order. Google uses WebKit as its browser in Android. (This application framework also powers Apple's Safari and Nokia's S60 browser.) Although WebKit does an adequate job of rendering complex Web pages, it can be slow at times.

The Droid browser

To use the Droid's Web browser, simply touch the aptly named Browser shortcut in the home screen. The browser displays a cached version of the last page you were browsing (or the Google home page, if you're using the app for the first time). To navigate to a Web page, just touch the search field at the top of the screen (**Figure 6.16**); type the Web address that you want to visit; and touch Go.

Figure 6.16
The Droid browser. To display the six options at the bottom of the screen, press the Menu button.

> **tip**   If you don't feel like typing, just touch the microphone icon to the right of the search field and simply speak your query. Google will transcribe your commands and execute a search. This feature isn't just cool; it's also revolutionary.

> **tip**   If you're not sure of the Web address, you can enter a search term in the search field, and you'll get search results from Google. You can also press the Search button (magnifying-glass icon) to do the same thing.

You have several ways to navigate a Web page, but I find the most convenient to be simply dragging a finger around on the touchscreen. When you're browsing a page that's too large for the Droid's screen (which isn't easy!), simply rotate it to use the wider landscape format. I find it a little easier to read long Web pages in landscape mode, but you should experiment with both portrait and landscape modes to see which works better for you.

If you're browsing a Web page that's not optimized for the small screen, touching anywhere on the screen displays two small magnifying-glass

icons at the bottom of the screen (**Figure 6.17**). As you've probably
guessed, you touch the plus (+) and minus (–) icons to zoom in and out of
a Web page, respectively.

Figure 6.17
*Viewing a Web
page gives you
two buttons
for zooming in
and out, but
multitouch is
much simpler.*

Zoom out   Zoom in

Google released a powerful new feature in Android 2.0 that's practically
a necessity: multitouch. *Multitouch* enables multiple-finger gestures on
the touchscreen, such as using two fingers to pinch-to-zoom on a photo.
This feature is much more intuitive and natural than the difficult zoom
icons, which don't work too well; multitouch is a breath of fresh air by
comparison.

note Initially, Google stayed away from multitouch because it feared a
patent skirmish with Apple over iOS. Then, in early 2010, Google
released a software update for the Nexus One that enabled pinch-to-zoom in its
Web browser, Google Maps app, and Gallery app. Apple blinked and didn't initiate any legal action over the move, and now multitouch is available in virtually
every Android app.

If the zoom icons and multitouch don't work for you, you can also double-tap anywhere on a Web page to zoom to a particular area for a closer look. Double-tapping is also nice because it zooms exactly the right amount and displays the paragraph or picture you double-tapped in full-screen view. When you're finished with a particular section, double-tap again to zoom out.

Shopping on the Run

When you're using the Browser app to search Google, you see a new icon to the right of the Search button: an icon that looks like a miniature bar code (**Figure 6.18**). If you touch this icon, you can download a free Android application called Barcode Scanner, which lets you use the Droid's camera to scan bar codes and then look up product information such as prices and reviews.

Figure 6.18
Tapping the mini bar-code icon to the right of the search field allows you to scan a bar code with your Droid's camera. Talk about cool!

Bar-code icon

Bookmarks, windows, and settings

The Android Web browser functions just like a desktop browser, right down to the bookmarks. Rather than touch the same Web address over and over, create a bookmark, which is much faster. To bookmark the page that you're viewing, touch Menu > More > Add Bookmark.

To navigate to a page that you've already bookmarked, press the Menu button and then touch Bookmarks at the bottom of the screen (refer to Figure 6.16 earlier in this chapter). The browser displays your bookmarks in reverse chronological order, including handy thumbnail images of the Web pages in question (**Figure 6.19**). To go to a bookmark, simply touch it.

Figure 6.19
Bookmarks view displays convenient thumbnail images.

If you're a power browser, having several browser windows open at the same time is convenient. Unfortunately, the Droid's screen isn't large enough for browser tabs. Instead, a built-in Windows feature allows you to navigate up to four Web pages quickly and easily (**Figure 6.20**). To access this feature, press the Menu button and then touch Windows at the bottom of the screen (refer to Figure 6.16 earlier in this chapter). Touch any page that you see in the Windows screen to go to that page, or touch the New Window option at the top of the screen to go to a different page.

Figure 6.20
The Windows screen lists all the Web pages that you have open.

Rounding out the browser's Menu-button options are Refresh, which reloads the page that you're viewing (which can be helpful when tickets are about to go on sale for Pearl Jam's 20th-anniversary festival); and More, which reveals navigation options and functions for sharing, bookmarking, and viewing a page's information (**Figure 6.21**).

Figure 6.21
Touching the Browser app's More option displays a litany of options, such as these.

Settings Galore

If you're into tweaking settings, you'll be in heaven when you touch Menu > More > Settings in the Android browser. The resulting Settings screen is easily the longest I've seen in any Android application (four scrolls!) and rivals the settings screen in most desktop browsers.

The first section, which covers the page-content settings, allows you to set the text size and things like pop-up blocking and loading images. For the most part, I leave these settings alone.

The second section focuses on privacy settings; it allows you to clear the cache, history, and cookies. The Remember Form Data option is extremely helpful, because it saves you from having to enter the same information (such as your user name and password) on pages that you visit frequently.

The Security section allows you to remember and clear passwords. (Saving form data isn't recommended for sensitive sites such as banking and e-commerce, because if you lose your phone, the person who finds it can look through your history and bookmarks, as well as log in to your accounts. Never save logins for sensitive sites on your Droid.)

The Advanced section allows you to enable and customize Google Gears. This app allows you to extend the browser's functionality by saving pages for offline viewing, which is eminently useful at times when you may be without Internet connectivity, such as during a commercial flight. Gears allows you to keep working when most people are forced to play solitaire.

7

Maps and Navigation

The advent of the portable GPS receiver (like the one in each Droid) means never having to use paper maps again—if you don't run out of battery charge, that is! With Google's free Maps and Navigation apps, you can determine your current location, find businesses and landmarks, view satellite and street-level images, and get turn-by-turn navigation with real-time traffic reports (**Figure 7.1** on the next page), all in the palm of your hand.

Maps and Navigation transform the Droid into a powerful navigation device that can replace the GPS receiver currently sitting on your dash. Make no mistake about it—executives at companies like Garmin, TomTom, and Magellan are paying very close attention to the explosion of GPS-equipped smartphones flooding the market.

Figure 7.1

Google Navigation is a full-featured navigation system that fits into your pocket.

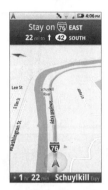

note Navigation requires Android 1.6 or later, and turn-by-turn voice guidance requires Android 2.0 or later.

Google Maps can even take advantage of the accelerometer built into the Droid to know which way you're holding or tilting the phone, which allows you to see not only your location—to an accuracy of about 10 feet (3 meters)—but also the actual direction in which you're facing.

In addition to the accelerometer, most Droids have a *magnetometer*, which is a fancy word for *compass*. The Droid's magnetometer knows which way you're facing, so instead of just looking at a static dot on a map, you'll see your "line of sight" turn as you turn around with your Droid. This feature is great for figuring out the direction you should walk in when you come out of the subway, for example.

The compass and gyroscope in the Droid gave birth to a whole new category of apps that use *augmented reality* (AR), which displays location-based information from Internet over a live video feed. A great example of AR in action is the free Sky Walk app, which allows you to locate the stars in the evening sky. If you haven't done it already, make sure to download this app right away. (More of my favorite apps are in Chapter 9.)

You'll probably use Google Maps for four main functions: finding locations, getting directions, navigating, and sharing your location. I cover each function in detail in this chapter. In addition, I give you a tour of the application's new, experimental Labs feature.

note As of February 2011, Navigation is available only in the United States, the United Kingdom, and parts of continental Europe. If you need global navigation, you can find several third-party navigation apps in the Android Market (Chapter 9).

Set Your Location

Before your Droid can harness the power of the orbiting GPS satellites, you have to give it explicit permission to do so. This permission requirement protects your privacy because (believe it or not) some people don't want to share their location information. To enable the Droid's GPS functionality, touch Settings > Location & Security to open the Location & Security Settings screen (**Figure 7.2**).

Figure 7.2

The My Location section of this screen allows you to toggle GPS on and off.

Then check the following boxes:

- **Use Wireless Networks.** This option uses cell towers and Wi-Fi networks to locate your phone. Although this option uses less battery power than the GPS option does, it's also less accurate than GPS.

- **Use GPS Satellites.** This option provides your location down to street level and is extremely accurate, but it also uses the most battery power of the three options in this group.

- **Enable Assisted GPS.** This option improves startup performance by using network resources to locate satellites faster and better when signal conditions are poor.

tip The Use GPS Satellites setting is extremely accurate, but the trade-off is that it uses a lot of battery power when it's enabled. If you need to conserve your battery, GPS is the first thing you should turn off.

Find a Location

Launch Google Maps by touching its icon on the home screen, and you'll see the last map you viewed. If you have GPS turned on, Maps will pinpoint your current location and display it on a map. You can display options at the bottom of the map when you press the Menu button (**Figure 7.3**), and you can find your current location very quickly by touching the gray bull's-eye icon in the top-right corner of the screen.

Figure 7.3
Six options are displayed when you press the Menu button.

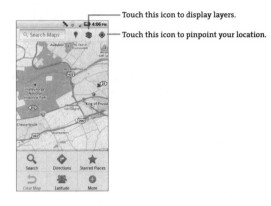

Touch this icon to display layers.

Touch this icon to pinpoint your location.

To find an address or city, touch Menu > Search. In the resulting screen (**Figure 7.4**), enter an address, business, or city, or simply touch the microphone icon and speak your query.

Figure 7.4
The search option in Maps also displays your search history.

Touch this icon to search by voice.

If you say "pizza," for example, Maps returns all the pizza shops near you, neatly plotted as a series of small red dots on your map. After touching one of the results, you get options to call the pizzeria's phone number, view its location on a map, get directions, or navigate to it. Pizza indeed! (I cover voice search in more detail in the next section.)

> **tip** When searching for an address that you've found before, you don't need to retype. Just type the first few letters and then choose the address from the list below the search box.

> **note** Google offers improved local business information, called Places, that appears in search results and includes things like store hours, prices, ratings, and reviews.

Voice search

Voice search is an extremely powerful feature that allows you to speak your destination instead of typing it. It employs the same core voice-search technology used throughout Android, which is best in class and accurate enough to be used as the primary interface to the device. I probably speak more search terms and addresses to my Droid than I type because speaking is faster and more convenient.

To use voice search, follow these steps:

1. Make sure that you have an Internet connection.

> **note** Speech recognition is done on the cloud, so you need an Internet connection to use voice search.

2. Touch the microphone icon (refer to Figure 7.4 earlier in this chapter), and say what you want to search for.

You could say something like "Navigate to Philadelphia International Airport," for example.

> **note** My experience has been that the Droid's speech recognition is excellent, understanding American, Australian, and British English. (At this writing, voice search is available only in English.)

When Maps finishes searching, it displays the result plotted on a map or—in the event of multiple choices—a list of results.

3. If the result shown onscreen is correct, follow the voice guidance; if you get multiple results, simply touch the proper result in the list and then follow the voice guidance.

 If accuracy isn't up to par, try again, speaking a little more slowly and clearly.

Voice actions

If you think voice search is cool, you'll love voice actions. In addition to searching, you can use voice actions to perform many other tasks quickly. Here are a few possibilities:

- Send text messages.
- Listen to music.
- Get directions.
- Call businesses.
- Call contacts.

- Send email.
- View a map.
- Go to Web sites.
- Say "Note to self..." to write a note (my favorite).

 Voice search for Android supports voice actions in Android 2.2 (Froyo) and later.

Layers

The Layers feature displays different types of data over a traditional Google map. To access it, touch the Maps icon and then touch the Layers icon in the top-right corner of the screen (refer to Figure 7.3 earlier in this chapter).

Figure 7.5 shows the Layers screen, which offers options including the following:

Figure 7.5

Layers allows you to choose how you want to view maps.

- **Traffic.** Traffic view displays real-time traffic conditions (where available) on the roads as color-coded lines. For more details on this feature, see the "Traffic" section later in this chapter.

- **Satellite.** This view superimposes actual satellite images on a traditional map, providing incredibly powerful information at your fingertips.

- **Latitude.** Latitude is one of Google's social-networking features that displays your friends' locations on a map. I cover this feature in "Share with Latitude" later in the chapter.

Touching the More Layers button (bottom of Figure 7.5) allows you to add even more layers for things like Wikipedia, Transit Lines, My Maps, and Favorite Places. Experiment with these options; they're a lot of fun. Just remember to come back and turn them off when you don't need them anymore; they can clutter a map quickly.

Get Directions

Google Maps for Droid includes several types of directions, including driving, public transportation, biking, and walking. I cover each of these direction types in the following sections and also discuss an important aspect of travel: traffic.

Driving

If you've used Google Maps on your desktop computer, using Maps' directions feature on your Droid will be second nature to you. To get driving directions, just follow these steps:

1. Touch the Maps shortcut on your home screen (or in the app tray).

2. Press the Menu button.

3. Touch the Directions option at the bottom of the screen (refer to Figure 7.3 earlier in this chapter).

4. Enter your starting and ending locations in the two fields at the top of the Directions screen (**Figure 7.6**).

Figure 7.6
Getting directions is as easy as entering two locations.

To save time, touch the square icon to the right of each address field to choose a location source. Your choices are My Current Location, Contacts, Point on Map, and Starred Places (**Figure 7.7**). Sure beats having to enter everything by hand!

Figure 7.7
*Choosing a
location source
instead of
entering it
saves time.*

5. Touch the icon for your mode of travel (in Figure 7.6, driving).

6. Touch Go.

   A new screen opens (**Figure 7.8**), giving you the option to view your destination on a map as a checkerboard pin, navigate to it (I cover navigation later in the chapter), or review the directions as a traditional text-based list.

Travel-mode   Show on Map
selector   button

Figure 7.8
Follow the
onscreen
directions or
touch Navigate
to get turn-by-
turn directions.

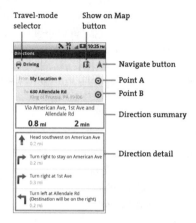

— Navigate button
— Point A
— Point B

— Direction summary

— Direction detail

Public transportation

Getting directions for taking public transportation (**Figure 7.9**) is just as
easy as getting them for driving a car. Just follow the procedure in the
"Driving" section, but instead of touching the car icon (refer to Figure 7.6)
in step 5, touch the bus icon. When you touch the Go button, Maps
routes you to your destination via available public transportation (trains,
subways, buses, and so on).

Figure 7.9
Maps even
provides transit
directions,
including
transfers.

Transit information isn't available everywhere, but I'm sure that Google is hard at work on expanding coverage. For more information on Google Maps for Transit, visit www.google.com/transit.

 tip Transit information is also available in Maps via a layer, which I cover in the "Layers" section earlier in this chapter.

Biking

In May 2010, Google added biking directions to its Maps app at the request of users and courtesy of the biking fanatics who work at Google. A team of brilliant gearheads combined Google's Maps app with bike-trail data, bike-lane information, and elevation data to provide routes tailored to cyclists. Maps automatically finds the most efficient and bike-friendly route by doing things like avoiding big hills and freeways. It even lets you customize your trip.

note The Terrain layer in Google Maps is as good as, or better than, topo-graphic maps from the U.S. Geological Survey. The detail and shading add a new dimension to your maps. Turn this feature on in the Layers screen (refer to Figure 7.5), and give Terrain a try!

Walking

Most city centers are a maze of one-way and no-left-turn streets, so traditional driving directions rarely show the most direct route for travel-ing by foot. That's where your Droid comes in handy. To get walking direc-tions, enter your start and end locations in the Directions screen (refer to Figure 7.6 earlier in this chapter), touch the pedestrian icon, and then touch the Go button.

Walking directions are even more convenient than you may think, especially for short trips in urban areas, but they aren't perfect. Google doesn't always know where the sidewalks are, for example, and construction crews always seem to be working on the roads in my area. As with any output from a computer, take walking directions with a grain of salt, and sanity-check them against your own experience and common sense.

Traffic

The Layers screen (refer to Figure 7.5 earlier in this chapter) offers you several ways to view your maps, but the Traffic layer is where the power of Google Maps really shines. When data is available, Google Maps provides live and predictive traffic information for all U.S. highways and secondary roads around the clock (**Figure 7.10**).

Figure 7.10
The Traffic layer indicates congestion by displaying green, yellow, and red lines on a map.

note   Green, yellow, and red traffic alerts don't translate well to a book that contains black-and-white images, so you'll have to test this feature on your own.

Google traffic information is based on past conditions and live crowd-sourcing, in which Maps users anonymously send their speed and location information to Google in the background. I provide more details on traffic in the following section.

If you checked the box to share your anonymous location data when your first launched Maps, pat yourself on the back. You put the "crowd" in crowdsourcing and are contributing to the real-time traffic information that Google displays in Maps. It's a noble cause, and you should be congratulated for it.

Navigate

Google Maps (**Figure 7.11**) provides free turn-by-turn GPS navigation with voice guidance, and it's Internet-connected to boot.

Figure 7.11

Google's free Navigation app is one of the best reasons to own a Droid.

Although it's getting mighty close, Google Navigation isn't a perfect replacement for a dedicated GPS receiver for heavy navigation users, such as salespeople and transportation companies. For starters, the Droid's 3.7- to 4.3-inch screen isn't as large as the screens in dedicated GPS units (which can measure 10 inches or more diagonally), and because all Droids are CDMA devices, they can't access the Internet (over 3G) while the user is making a voice call. If you need to be able to make phone calls while using navigation, a dedicated automotive GPS receiver may be more your speed.

Constant Internet connection

Being Internet-connected all the time means that you always have access to the latest Google Maps data on your Droid.

Traditional GPS devices come with maps that were installed at the factory. If you purchase a GPS receiver in 2011, it could have maps from 2010 or 2009 installed—and if you bought the device at a deep-discount or closeout sale, or bought it used, the maps may be from (shudder!) 2008. It sounds silly, but it's important to have up-to-date maps, because

- Roads and subdivisions are always being closed, changed, or repaired (seemingly at the most inopportune times!).

- Business data—known as *points of interest* (POIs) in GPS parlance— is best served fresh. Although it may be inconvenient to find out that a road has been changed, it's much more inconvenient to discover that the gas station that you just navigated to closed years ago.

tip **Fresh local data is especially important for making a dinner reservation, because restaurants tend to turn over faster than other businesses do. You're more likely to get disconnected numbers and empty parking lots if your data is more than a year old.**

Google Maps on your Droid is pulling data from the same giant database as good old Google.com on your desktop computer, so when you search for, say, a mechanic or emergency services, you can be sure that you have the most up-to-date information possible.

tip **If the navigation features included in Google Maps are too pedestrian (pun intended) for you, you can find several more navigation apps in the Android Market (see Chapter 9). Be warned, though: Most third-party navigation apps aren't free.**

Traffic detection and avoidance

Google Maps can display real-time traffic data overlaid on maps in a simple green, yellow, and red color scheme. As with traffic lights, green means go (no traffic), yellow means slow down (some traffic), and red means stop (heavy traffic). To get details on an area, touch it to zoom out to an aerial view that shows traffic speeds and incidents ahead.

Maps gathers its traffic data via crowdsourcing, analyzing the speed and location data sent by other users and turning that data into easy-to-read traffic data that benefits all users.

In addition to showing you traffic that's coming up on your route (detection), Maps can help you detour around it (avoidance). When the app finds traffic on your route, it displays an alternative-route icon at the bottom of the screen (**Figure 7.12**). Touch that icon to display a new route around the traffic ahead.

Figure 7.12
The alternative-route icon allows you to detour around traffic.

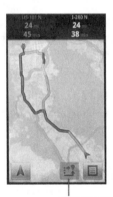

Alternative-route icon

note For mission-critical routes to doctors and hospitals, it never hurts to (ahem!) get a second opinion.

Satellite layer

The Satellite layer is one of Google Maps' most powerful features. It shows actual satellite imagery of your route, helping put it in context by displaying landmarks like parks, buildings, and bodies of water.

To enable this feature, simply touch the Layers icon (refer to Figure 7.3 earlier in this chapter), or touch Menu > Layers and then touch Satellite. Instead of seeing a boring line-art map devoid of detail, you'll see a view of your location as only a satellite can show it (**Figure 7.13**). Don't forget to use two-finger gestures like pinch to zoom to explore the Satellite layer.

Figure 7.13

Satellite view is more useful on a smartphone than on a desktop computer.

Satellite view won't clog the precious storage on your Droid; all the data is downloaded on demand from Google via your Internet connection. Jack Bauer would be proud.

Street View

Street View (**Figure 7.14** on the next page) allows you to take a virtual drive or walk down most major U.S. streets, thanks to street-level photos that Google has painstakingly collected and mapped to GPS coordinates.

The result is fantastically useful for finding a specific personal or business destination, scouting locations for a trip or film, or even finding a new home—all without leaving your current zip code.

Figure 7.14
*Street View can
be amazingly
helpful on a
Droid.*

Although some other GPS receivers show you an artist's rendering of a particular road or street sign, Google Maps on the Droid shows you actual street-level photos of your route so that you can plan your next turn easily (or find a place to park). When you arrive at your destination, Maps also shows you a Street View of the location, making sure that you arrive at the right place and not at the building next door.

Street View is available on desktop computers, but it becomes even more powerful when it's used on a mobile device like the Droid. It's one thing to use Street View to scout a hotel before you book a room from your office PC, but it's even more useful when you're walking around trying to find the location of your business meeting (with your Droid, of course!).

Car-dock mode

If you're going to use Google Maps in your vehicle (and who wouldn't?), you should make one additional purchase: a good car dock that lets you safely mount your Droid on your vehicle's windshield. Having a car dock beats having a Droid slide across your dashboard; trust me on that one.

All you need is a suction-cup mounting bracket with the appropriate snap-in bracket for your Droid (around $30). When you snap your Droid into the mount, the device switches to car-dock mode (**Figure 7.15**). Alternatively, you can touch Car Dock in the app tray.

Figure 7.15
Car-dock mode turns the Droid into a full-fledged personal navigation device.

Car-dock mode is an excellent software feature that optimizes the Droid's interface for arm's-length control, displaying large icons that are easy to read (and touch) from a distance. It also boils the Droid interface down to five main tasks:

- Music
- My Location
- Calling
- Add App
- Voice Search

The single best feature of car-dock mode is voice search. As I discuss in copious detail elsewhere in this chapter and book, voice search allows you to speak instead of type your query. Nowhere is this type of feature more valuable than in car-dock mode, because when you're driving, you should have your hands on the wheel and your eyes on the road.

To use it, simply touch the Voice Search icon, and when you're prompted, say a phrase like "Navigate to California Pizza Kitchen" (**Figure 7.16**). Maps displays that phrase and maps your route. If it heard you right, that's all you have to do. If the text onscreen isn't what you said, touch the Cancel icon and try again.

Figure 7.16
Simply speak your destination to navigate in car-dock mode.

Voice-activated features aren't infallible, because they can be adversely affected by things like background noise, but after you get used to them, there's simply no going back. What could be easier than speaking to your computer or phone?

Share with Latitude

Google Maps is handy for more than just viewing maps and providing directions; it's also excellent for sharing your current location with friends. Sharing is the basis of a whole new category of social-networking applications, and Google is joining the party with its own entry.

Google Latitude (www.google.com/latitude) is a social-networking service that plots your friends' locations on a map (**Figure 7.17**)—a handy way to see who's out and about. With it, you can text, instant-message, or call any of your friends who are nearby. This feature is only as good as the number of your friends who use it, so to make it successful, you need to invite your friends to share your data and hope that they reciprocate.

Figure 7.17
With Latitude, it's easy to see when your friends are in the area.

note If you're concerned about stalkers, keep in mind that Latitude is an opt-in feature, which means that *you* turn it on and *you* determine who can see your location. For obvious reasons, exercise a lot of discretion in sharing your location information, and grant access only to your closest friends.

To participate in Latitude, you need to join. To do so, touch Menu > Join Latitude; then touch Menu > Add Friends, and select people from your contacts list or add people's email addresses manually. When you're done, those people will receive an email invitation to Latitude.

note You can remove a friend by long-pressing his or her name and then touching Remove This Friend in the resulting list.

Sharing your location . . .

Latitude periodically asks you to share your location details with another user. When it does, you have three choices:

- **Accept and Share Back.** When you choose this option, you can see your friends' locations, and they can see yours.

- **Accept, but Hide My Location.** This option lets you see your friends' locations but blocks them from seeing yours.

- **Don't Accept.** You can't see your friends, and they can't see you.

. . . or not

You can stop publishing your location information to your Latitude friends at any time by touching Menu > Privacy in the main Latitude screen. This screen gives you four options:

- **Detect Your Location.** This option (the default) updates your location automatically.

- **Set Your Location.** When you choose this option, you set your location on the map manually.

- **Hide Your Location.** Choose this option, and your friends can't see your location.

- **Turn off Latitude.** When you turn off Latitude, you can't see or be seen.

Experiment with Labs

Although the name conjures images of serious-looking academics in lab coats using Bunsen burners (at least, it does for me), Labs is a fun experimental area of Google where programmers are allowed to test new software on us. Wait a minute—they're experimenting on us! Stop the presses!

Seriously, the Labs feature of Google Maps has some great features that are tucked away just waiting to be used, and I'm baffled as to why they're not in the main screen. To view them (**Figure 7.18**), touch Menu > More > Labs.

Figure 7.18

Lurking in Maps are some experimental features that are quite useful.

note As with anything new, experimental, or from Google, expect Labs to change. The features that I discuss in the following sections were available on my Droid X in February 2011. Depending on when you read this chapter, Labs may also have an option to make you a sandwich, too!

Scale bar

The Scale Bar option displays a scale (both imperial and metric units) in the bottom-left corner of a map. It's really useful for telling the distance between two locations, especially if you zoom in and out of maps frequently.

Measure

Checking this option adds a new onscreen button that acts like a tape measure, allowing you to measure the distance between points on your map (**Figure 7.19**). It's super-useful for planning your next hike, mountain-bike ride, or snowmobiling trip.

Figure 7.19

The little measuring-tape button lets you see the distance between two points.

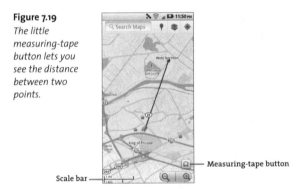

Measuring-tape button

Scale bar

tip Maps has almost limitless applications over and beyond those listed in this chapter. Be sure to check out Chapter 9 for some of the creative ways that developers are using GPS technology in new apps.

The Best Part: Price

The best part about all this wonderful map technology is its price. It's *completely free*, in that it's included in the cost of your Droid and monthly data plan. I can't emphasize enough how important this fact is. Think about all the recurring monthly bills that you pay now: Internet access, mobile-phone plan, Starbucks card, and so on. They add up. The last thing you probably need is another monthly payment (or, even worse, another deduction from your checking account).

Although traditional GPS receivers freely use the circling government satellites to plot your location and help you navigate, many companies charge extra for add-on features such as traffic, weather, and sports scores. Also, don't forget the annual fees that some GPS providers charge for upgrading the maps on your GPS device, which can run about $50 per year. And don't get me started on how long it takes to load updated maps onto a GPS receiver.

Because you own a Droid, all these features are included in your plan. This fact alone must be creating problems for GPS manufacturers; it's sure to cost them customers as people migrate to phone-based navigation, especially because the Droid's free service is feature-rich and doesn't require a dedicated GPS device.

That was a lot of technology to digest. In Chapter 8, I take a bit of a breather from the heavy technical jargon and have some fun reviewing some of the most entertaining aspects of the Droid: its multimedia apps.

8

Fun with Media

The past several chapters are rather utilitarian, focusing on tools like email, messaging, and contacts. Now it's time to let your hair down a little. In this chapter, I run down all the multimedia options that are available on the Droid, including photos, music, and movies. Let's have some fun, shall we?

note Numerous third-party apps that play (and record) multimedia are available from the Android Market. This chapter focuses on the apps that are preinstalled on the Droid; I cover third-party apps and the Android Market in Chapter 9.

Camera

A very useful feature of most modern smartphones is its built-in camera. It's incredibly convenient to be able to whip out your phone and snap a photo on demand. Because you always have your phone with you (at least, I do), it's easy to take a quick photo of the kids playing at the park—and the Internet access makes the Droid's camera even more powerful.

Instead of just shooting and storing photos for a rainy day, you can easily fire off an email to Nanny and Pop from the park. Sending camera-phone photos by MMS is especially useful for communicating something that's hard to describe in words. These pictures are a great way to get an absent someone's opinion of an appliance or piece of furniture, for example. (See Chapter 6 for more about MMS.)

Smartphone cameras have a reputation for poor image quality, but this reputation is proving to be a myth as technology continues to improve.

Droids come with an impressive 5- to 8-megapixel autofocus camera with a dual-LED flash and 720p video recording (depending on your model). In fact, Droids have all the bells and whistles of a modern digital camera, including image stabilization; white-balance control; fun features like geotagging; image editing; color effects; and built-in scene settings for things like sunset, snow, and beach. Holy Ansel Adams!

note **The Droid X packs three microphones that behave differently depending on whether you're using the phone, speakerphone, or video camera. Each mic can be used for audio capture and for noise cancellation, depending on the situation. Cool, huh?**

Taking photos

Taking photos with your Droid's camera is definitely an art, and getting it right takes a little practice. If you're patient and have a steady hand, however, the output from the Droid's camera can be quite impressive.

To take a photo on the Droid, follow these steps:

1. Launch the Camera app by touching the Camera icon in the app tray or (Droid X only) the Camera key on the edge of the device.

2. Review the onscreen information (**Figure 8.1**).

Figure 8.1

The Camera app is basically a giant viewfinder with a shutter-release button.

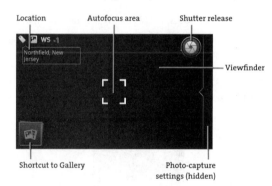

Location   Autofocus area   Shutter release

Northfield, New Jersey

Viewfinder

Shortcut to Gallery   Photo-capture settings (hidden)

3. Frame your subject with the viewfinder.

   You can hold the Droid horizontally or vertically.

4. Press the onscreen shutter-release button or hardware shutter-release key.

   If your Droid has a hardware key, first press it halfway down to focus; then press it all the way down to take the photo.

tip Try to keep your Droid as still as possible when taking photos. A slight lag occurs between the time when you press the shutter release and the time when the Droid actually captures the photo, making it difficult to photograph kids, pets, and other fast-moving objects. For best results, try to keep your hands—and your subjects—still for a full second after you press the shutter release.

Pictures taken with the Droid's camera are automatically saved to the Gallery app, which I cover later in this chapter.

Reviewing photos

To review your photos, simply touch the thumbnail image in the corner of the onscreen viewfinder. The image viewer opens, displaying the most recent photo taken.

Pressing the Menu button while you're in this screen displays six options (**Figure 8.2**):

Figure 8.2
Several options are available when you're reviewing an image.

- **Camera.** Touch this option to switch back to camera mode.

- **Quick Upload.** Touch this option to automatically upload a photo to a service you're already set up (such as Facebook, Twitter, Photobucket, or Picasa).

- **Share.** The Share button allows you to send a photo immediately via email, text message, Dropbox, or just about any photo-sharing service.

 The list you see when you touch the Share button depends on what accounts you have configured.

- **Edit.** This option allows you to add tags, rotate, resize, crop, and perform several other adjustments on photos.

- **Delete.** Touch this button to trash photos that are blurry or poorly composed.

- **More.** This option reveals a submenu that allows you to print; use a photo as a contact, profile, or desktop picture; and even adjust the Gallery settings.

Camera settings

While you're using the Camera app, touching the right edge of the screen (refer to Figure 8.1 earlier in this chapter) reveals several camera settings (**Figure 8.3**):

Figure 8.3
The Camera app has a few settings that are tucked away until you need them.

- **Scenes.** One of my favorite Camera-app features, Scenes mode allows you to choose a setting that optimizes the camera for the type of photo you're taking. Your options are Auto (the default), Portrait, Landscape, Sport, Night Portrait, Sunset, Macro, and Steady Shot.

- **Effects.** Touching this option lets you apply one of several color effects to your photos, including Black and White; Negative; Sepia; Solarize; and Red, Blue, and Green tints. The default setting is Normal, which applies none of these effects.

- **Flash.** This option allows you to choose among On, Off, and Auto (the default).

- **Switch To.** This option (obscured by the Settings button in Figure 8.3) allows you to switch quickly between still and video shooting.

Pressing the Menu button reveals three more buttons (bottom of Figure 8.3)— Picture Modes, Tags, and Settings—that allow you to adjust photo and video resolution, album uploading, review time, face detection, ISO-equivalent sensitivity, exposure, and shutter animation.

Shooting video

With the release of the Android 2.0 operating system, the Droid's Camera app gained the ability to shoot DVD-quality video: 720p x 480p video at 24 frames per second (fps). It also captures AAC audio in the process, so you won't be stuck with silent movies.

You don't want to toss your high-definition handycam just yet, however. The Droid's size limits the space available for the video sensor and associated electronics, so it's important to have realistic expectations. On the other hand, the Droid is a very capable camcorder and one of the most "pocketable" video cameras around.

note The Droid X includes an HDMI port for viewing content on an external screen. All you need is a type-D HDMI cable (about $10) to make the connection. You can play photos and videos from the Gallery app, stream movies from the Blockbuster app, or even play DivX movies on an external HDMI display.

To shoot a video on the Droid, follow these steps:

1. Launch the Camera app by touching its icon in the app tray.

> **tip** If your Droid has a hardware shutter-release key, you can launch Camera simply by pressing and holding that key.

2. Touch Switch To in the bottom-right corner of the screen to switch to video recording.

3. Frame your subject, using the onscreen viewfinder.

4. Press the Droid's hardware Camera key or touch the red shutter-release button in the top-right corner of the screen to start and stop recording.

> **tip** Numerous third-party apps extend the camera's functionality well beyond photos and movies. Some apps, for example, allow the camera to scan a product bar code and return comparison prices from the Internet. Read about some of the best Android apps in Chapter 9.

Gallery

Gallery is the companion app to Android's Camera app; it manages the photos and video that you shoot with your Droid. Launch Gallery by touching its icon in the app tray, and you'll see the image browser (**Figure 8.4** on the next page). The thumbnail images represent all the photos and videos that you've shot on the Droid, as well as any that you've transferred to your Droid's microSD card.

Figure 8.4

The Gallery app's image browser, here showing photos grouped by tag.

By default, the browser is organized into four main sections: Camera Roll, My Tags, Folder, and All Photos. Touch any of the stacks to reveal a thumbnail gallery of up to 24 photos (**Figure 8.5**). Flick your finger up and down the screen to scroll through the photos.

Figure 8.5

Thumbnail view allows you to scroll through your photos and videos quickly.

Viewing photos

To see a photo in full-screen mode, touch its thumbnail in the image browser. When you're in full-screen mode, touch anywhere on the screen to display small option icons (**Figure 8.6**). Depending on your model, these options are HDMI Out (Droid X and Bionic), Slideshow, and Info.

Figure 8.6
Several options are available while you're viewing an image.

— HDMI Out

— Slideshow
— Info

Touching the Info icon opens a small window that gives you detailed information about the current photo (**Figure 8.7**).

Figure 8.7
Touching a photo's Info button displays all kinds of useful information.

To navigate among photos in full-screen mode, simply swipe your finger across the screen horizontally. To zoom in or out, use two fingers to pinch the screen. You can also double-tap an area to zoom in and double-tap again to zoom out.

Sharing photos

After you've built up a library of photos (and if you're like me, this won't take long), you can have some real fun with them. It's not much fun to keep all your photos bottled up in your Droid, so why not share them with friends in the moment? You don't need to wait to get home from a trip to share your photos; send a photo of your kids at the beach *from* the beach.

When you're in full-screen mode, press the Menu button to display photo options (refer to Figure 8.2 earlier in this chapter) and then touch the More button to reveal the options shown in **Figure 8.8**.

Figure 8.8
Press Menu and then touch More to access additional photo options.

These options are

- **Set As.** The Set As option allows you to set the photo as a contact icon or as your phone's wallpaper.

- **Print.** Don't get too excited. As of Android 2.2.1, this option lets you print a photo at a retail destination (such as Walgreens or CVS)—not on your printer at home.

- **Settings.** Touching this option brings up the Gallery Settings screen (**Figure 8.9**), which lets you tweak the behavior of slideshows as follows:

  - **Slideshow Interval.** Sets how long each slide is displayed.

  - **Repeat Slideshow.** Repeats your slideshow in a loop.

  - **Shuffle Slides.** Displays your photos in random order.

  - **Slideshow Transition.** Sets the effect that you want to use between slides.

  - **Quick Upload Album.** Sets which service will be used for the default upload account.

  - **Tag with Contacts.** Autocompletes tags with contact names. (I prefer to leave this option turned off because short names are easier to view than full names from my contacts list.)

Figure 8.9

The Gallery Settings screen allows you to adjust various slideshow settings.

Music

Now that you're an expert at taking photos and videos with your Droid, it's time to relax with some music. In addition to being a capable phone and camera, the Droid makes a great jukebox.

Before you start jamming on your Droid, you need to transfer some music to it. All music on the Droid is stored on its microSD card, which goes in the expansion-card slot. The Music app won't run unless a microSD card is installed.

 Although the 16 GB card included with your Droid is quite capable and should last a while, it will eventually fill up. Luckily, additional 16 GB and 32 GB cards are relatively inexpensive.

Android's Music app supports the following audio file formats:

- AAC, AAC+, and eAAC+ (.3gp, .mp4, .m4a)
- MP3 (.mp3)
- MIDI (.mid and others)
- Ogg Vorbis (.ogg)

Sorry, Windows Media fans—the Droid has no WMA support.

note **To see how to transfer music to your Droid, flip to "Transferring files" later in this chapter.**

Playing music

When you launch the Music app by touching its icon in the app tray, you see the main Music interface, which is neatly divided into four logical tabs that organize your music by artists, albums, songs, and playlists. If you can't find what you're looking for, press the Menu button and then touch Search in the resulting list of options. Alternatively, if you're not in the mood to think, press Menu and then touch Party Shuffle to play randomly selected tunes.

Artists tab

The Artists tab (**Figure 8.10**) displays all the music on your memory card sorted by artist. Flick up and down to scroll. Touch any artist's name to drill down to all the songs by that artist, and touch a song to start playing it.

Figure 8.10

The Music app's Artists tab. Touch the little arrow button next to an artist's name to display all the albums by that artist.

While a song is playing, a gray Now Playing strip at the bottom of the screen provides some basic information about the song. Touching that strip takes you to the Now Playing screen, which I cover later in this chapter.

Albums tab

The Albums tab (**Figure 8.11** on the next page) displays your music sorted by album. This view is helpful when you have a lot of complete albums, but it can get long when you have a mishmosh of music or a bunch of music in one particular genre. Albums view displays the album artwork (assuming that you have it), album name, and artist for each piece of music that you have loaded on your memory card.

Figure 8.11

The Music app's Albums tab.

Songs tab

The Songs tab (**Figure 8.12**) is also pretty self-explanatory, displaying every song loaded on your memory card. Below each song name is the artist's name, and to the right is the song's running time. Simply touch any song to play it, or flick your finger up and down the screen until you find something that you like.

Figure 8.12

The Music app's Songs tab.

tip One of my favorite things to do in Songs view is flick-shuffle, which involves giving the song list a good flick with my finger and then randomly touching the screen to stop at a song. Think of this technique as being like spinning that big wheel in the Showcase Showdown on "The Price Is Right," except that you don't have to wait for the wheel to stop.

Playlists view

Finally, you can view your music by playlist (**Figure 8.13**) when you touch the Playlists tab at the top of the main Music screen. The Droid supports .m3u playlists, which it reads from the microSD card.

note An .m3u file is a text file that contains the location of media files. Your music-player software reads the .m3u file to see what order to play the media files in.

Figure 8.13
The Music app's Playlists tab.

If you want to use playlists, create a Playlists folder inside the Music folder on your memory card, and copy your .m3u files to it. After you do, your playlists will show up whenever you touch the Playlists tab.

tip You can create a playlist directly on the Droid by long-pressing any song and touching Add to Playlist > New. You can also play, delete, or rename a playlist just by long-pressing it.

Now Playing

When a song is playing, you can get to the Now Playing screen by touching the gray strip at the bottom of any of the Music app's various screens. This screen displays the album art associated with the current track and a set of controls (**Figure 8.14**).

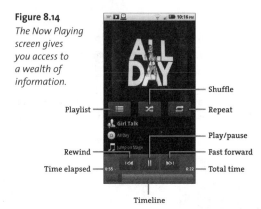

Figure 8.14
The Now Playing screen gives you access to a wealth of information.

Playlist

Shuffle

Repeat

Play/pause

Rewind

Fast forward

Time elapsed

Total time

Timeline

Transferring files

Moving photos, videos, and music (and all other files, for that matter) between your Droid and a desktop computer is easy. Just follow these steps:

1. Connect your Droid to any PC or Mac with the included USB cable.

   When it's connected, your Droid will display a USB icon in the status bar.

2. Drag the status bar down to reveal the notification window, and touch USB Connected.

3. Touch Mount.

Your Droid's SD card will appear in My Computer (Windows) or on the Desktop (Mac).

4. Transfer the files via drag and drop or copy and paste.

5. Pull down the status bar to reveal the notifications window, and touch Turn off USB Storage.

6. Unplug the USB cable, and you're done!

tip Another way to transfer files to the Droid is to insert the microSD card into an SD card carrier and then insert the carrier into a card reader connected to your computer. At that point, you can copy the files to the card.

note You can keep tabs on how much space is available on your Droid's microSD card by touching Settings > SD Card & Phone Storage. Other options allow you to unmount and format your microSD card.

More Than Music

You can also use music and audio files from your computer as alarms, notifications, and ringtones on the Droid. Simply create folders named Alarms, Notifications, and Ringtones at the root level of the microSD card; then copy the appropriate files to the correct folders. The next time you set an alarm, notification, or ringtone, you'll see your music files as choices. Cool!

YouTube for Mobile

YouTube enjoys more than 2 billion views per day, and it would take more than 1,700 years to watch its entire library of videos. Because Google owns YouTube *and* develops Android, it's only logical that the Droid ships with a native YouTube app.

Navigating the app

The bundled YouTube for Mobile app gives your Droid access to a huge catalog of videos that you can search by keyword or browse by category. As you'd expect, the user interface (**Figure 8.15**) is dead simple to use: Just flick your finger up and down the screen to scroll through the most popular and suggested videos.

Figure 8.15
The main YouTube app interface, with menu options displayed.

Each video has a thumbnail image that displays its length, and to the right of the image are the video's name, uploader, and source. Just touch a video to play it and read its comments. If you want to search, touch the magnifying-glass icon in the top-right corner of the screen, and if you want to record and upload a video, touch the camera icon next to it.

Pressing the Menu button reveals six options (refer to Figure 8.15):

- **Home.** Returns you to the main YouTube screen.

- **Browse**. Displays a list of the 15 most popular categories of videos, including Music, People & Blogs, and Science & Technology.

- **Search.** Allows you to search for videos by keywords or phrases. (For a good laugh, try searching for *"michael jackson brazil taxi driver".*)

- **My Channel.** Lets you view your uploads, favorites, playlists, and subscriptions when you're logged in to your YouTube account. (See the nearby sidebar for more information.)

- **Upload.** Lets you upload videos to YouTube from the Gallery app (refer to "Gallery" earlier in this chapter) or a third-party video app.

- **Settings.** Allows you to clear your search history, filter videos by time, and read YouTube's terms-of-service agreement.

My Channel

If you touch Menu > My Channel in the YouTube for Mobile app, you'll be able to log in to your YouTube account from the My Channel screen (**Figure 8.16**). This screen also lets you view statistical information about your uploaded videos and browse your favorites and playlists. You can even view and manage your YouTube subscriptions from the Subscriptions tab (hidden to the right of the Playlists tab in Figure 8.16).

Figure 8.16 *Logging in to your YouTube account allows you to view information about your videos.*

Watching videos

The Droid's stunning screen makes it one of the best smartphones for watching videos. By default, YouTube videos play in high-quality mode on the Droid when you're using Wi-Fi (see Chapter 3). If you're out of Wi-Fi range, you can still watch videos in high definition by touching Menu > Settings > High Quality on Mobile, although they'll take slightly longer to load.

The controls of the YouTube for Mobile app are much like those in the desktop version of YouTube, allowing you to search, share, rate, comment on, and view videos on the go.

Watching a video is as simple as touching its thumbnail image. You can watch it vertically with info below it or rotate your Droid to landscape mode for a full-screen viewing experience. From that point on, the YouTube for Mobile app works pretty much the same way as the VCR you bought more than 20 years ago. Play, fast-forward, and rewind, baby!

Uploading videos

Because the Droid allows you to shoot DVD-quality video (as I discuss in "Shooting video" earlier in this chapter), you can upload your videos directly to YouTube from the phone. The Droid's capability to add effects such as solarization and tints to your videos will channel your inner Martin Scorsese before you know it.

tip **The YouTube widget (accessible by long-pressing the YouTube icon in the home screen and then touching Widgets) gives you easy access to recording and sharing capabilities right from your Droid's home screen.**

So there you have it. Take some time to learn the lighter side of Android. It can be great to share your photos, unwind to some tunes, and get a quick laugh courtesy of a video on YouTube.

Now that I've covered most of the included apps on Android, it's time to cast a wider net. In Chapter 9, I give you an overview of the Android Market, a wonderful resource where you can choose among thousands of apps.

9

Android Market

The most fun and powerful feature of the Droid is the Android Market. It's fun because it offers so many types of apps—something for everyone—and it's powerful because it contains more than 200,000 apps. Although its catalog may not be as deep as those of other app stores, the Android Market is a formidable challenger in the white-hot apps race.

Check out these Market milestones in the number of apps available for download:

- March 2009: 2,300
- November 2009: 12,000
- December 2009: 20,000
- December 2010: 200,000 (a tenfold increase in one year!)

The Market is a fast-growing treasure chest of goodies for owners of Droids, and it's getting better all the time, as Android has matured into an enticing platform for developers of Android apps.

In this chapter, I show you how to use the Android Market and highlight some of the best apps that I've found.

note This chapter covers Android Market 2.2.6, which has many new features, including the capability to discover apps on your desktop computer and push them to your Android phone. (Very cool!) Be sure to update to the latest version of the Market if you're using an older version.

Navigating the Market

The Market app comes preinstalled on all Android-powered phones. To launch it, simply touch the Market shortcut on your home screen or in the app tray. (It's the one with the friendly robot on a shopping bag.) Like most apps for Android, the Market has a dead-simple interface. When you launch it, you're greeted by a tidy, well-organized, easy-to-navigate screen (**Figure 9.1**).

Figure 9.1

The Android Market's home screen.

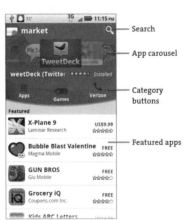

- Search
- App carousel
- Category buttons
- Featured apps

The home screen gives you several ways to navigate the sea of apps that awaits you:

- **Search.** The magnifying-glass icon in the top-right corner of the screen is a good way to get an app fast. Just touch it and type a few words in the search field. For more info, see "Searching for Apps" later in this chapter.

- **App carousel.** Front and center is the app carousel—a revolving door of app icons designed to entice you and pique your interest.

- **Category buttons.** Across the top of the main Market screen is a navigation bar containing three buttons:

    - **Apps.** Touching the Apps button reveals a catch-all list of categories, such as Books & Reference, Business, Comics, and Communication. Touch a category to see a list of all the apps in that category, sortable by top paid, top free, and just in.

    - **Games.** This area of the Market is for the gamer in you. Touch the Games button to reveal numerous categories, from Arcade & Action to Brain & Puzzle.

    - **Verizon.** Because the Droid is exclusive to Verizon Wireless, the carrier gets its own button in the Market. Touching the Verizon button displays a screen of apps designed or distributed by that carrier, including NFL Mobile, Skype Mobile, and MyVerizon.

- **Featured apps.** In this section, you see an app's icon and name, the developer's name, the price, and the user rating. Slide your finger up and down the screen to scroll through the list. Touching any of the featured apps takes you to the detail-view screen for that app.

 Google updates this section of the Market regularly, so it's a good idea to check in periodically to see what's new.

An app's detail-view screen (**Figure 9.2**) displays a wealth of information, which varies depending on its download status. If the app you're browsing (in Figure 9.2, Angry Birds Seasons) is already installed on your Droid, you'll see Open and Uninstall buttons for it, as well as an Allow Automatic Updating option (which I enable for a few of my primary apps that I always want to keep up to date). You can also rate it based on a five-star scale.

Figure 9.2
The detail-view screen allows you to do your research before installing an app from the Market.

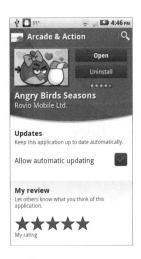

If you haven't installed the app, you'll see a large Install (if it's free) or Buy (if it's paid) button at the bottom of the screen.

In all detail-view screens, you can scroll down to see a description, screen shots, reviews, related apps, and developer information.

Searching for Apps

You'd probably guess that any product coming from a company like Google would have amazing search capabilities, right? Well, you'd be wrong. Although it's gotten easier recently, searching the Android Market can be challenging.

A search in the Android Market for "*golf*", for example, yielded 460 results in February 2011, up from 71 a year earlier. The results included golf games (well, duh!), apps for keeping score and for tracking your position on the course via GPS, golf news, travel and trivia apps, and (of course) golf jokes. If you think that 460 is a lot of golf apps, searching for "*twitter*" produced 4,874 results (**Figure 9.3**).

Figure 9.3

Searching for "twitter" nets more than 4,000 results.

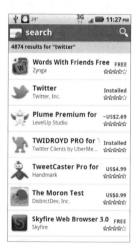

The best way to combat search fatigue is to use a specific search phrase, such as "*twitter multiple accounts.*" This phrase returns a more manageable 51 results, listing Twitter clients that support multiple accounts.

If I can't find what I'm looking for in the Market on my Droid, I usually opt to search the Android Market Web site (http://market.android.com) on my computer. Search is a little faster when you can enter search terms on a full-size keyboard.

tip Try searching the names of some of your hobbies or interests, and you'll probably find some interesting selections. Or search for *"Android"* plus a few keywords.

Installing Apps

note You need a Google Checkout account to buy apps from the Android Market. If you don't have an account, you can set one up at www. google.com/checkout.

Purchasing an app in the Android Market is actually quite easy. Here's all you have to do:

1. Launch the Market (if it isn't already running) by touching its shortcut in the home screen.

2. Find the app you want to install, following the directions in the preceding section.

3. Touch the app's icon to open its detail-view screen (refer to Figure 9.2 earlier in this chapter).

4. Touch either the Buy button (for paid apps) or the Install button (for free apps) at the top of the screen.

5. Touch OK to accept permissions (**Figure 9.4**).

    The app downloads to your Droid.

Figure 9.4

Before installing an app, you have to accept its permissions, which vary widely by app.

Read the Fine Print Before Buying

When you've found an app that you want to purchase, consider a few things before touching the Buy button:

- **Reinstallations.** The Android Market allows you to reinstall purchased apps an unlimited number of times at no charge. This feature comes in handy when you get a new Android device or when a factory reset is necessary.

- **Returns.** The Market accepts returns within 15 minutes of purchase (not download). The clock starts ticking the moment you purchase an app, not whenever you get around to installing it, so you should try to use a new app immediately after buying it. You may return a given app only one time; if you purchase the same app again later, you can't return it a second time.

- **Billing disputes.** Google is not responsible for billing disputes arising from Android Market purchases. All billing issues should be directed to the developer in question, the payment processor, or your credit-card company, as appropriate.

Market returns are handled directly in each app. Just touch the icon for the app in question and then touch Uninstall & Refund. If the refund option isn't there, your 24-hour return window has passed.

Updating Apps

Developers frequently release updates to their apps to add features and fix bugs. When an update is available for an Android Market app that you've already downloaded, your Droid displays a notification icon in the status bar. Expose the status bar, touch Updates Available, and follow the prompts to install the updates.

You can easily keep your apps up to date by launching the Market app and touching Menu > My Apps. The resulting My Apps screen (**Figure 9.5**) lists all the apps that you've downloaded to date. Apps that have pending updates appear at the top of the screen, with *Update* displayed next to their names in red. To install an update, just touch the app; then touch Update, followed by the OK button. Updates are downloaded simultaneously and in the background, allowing you to use other apps while they download.

 Touch the new Update All button at the top of the My Apps screen to update all your apps in one fell swoop.

Figure 9.5

The My Apps screen makes it easy to keep all your apps current.

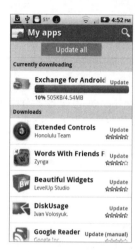

Introducing My App Hall of Fame

With more than 200,000 apps (and counting) available in the Android Market, it can be difficult to find the gems—which is where this section of the chapter comes in. Here are some of the most interesting apps that I've discovered in my travels around the Market, listed in no particular order. Some are free, and some are paid (as noted); all of them are useful, entertaining, or both.

This list is designed to get you started down the wonderful path of app discovery. Use it to jump-start your own app collection, and you'll soon be exploring the endless possibilities that exist courtesy of your Droid and the Android Market.

Google Voice

Price: Free

Developer: Google (www.google.com/mobile/voice)

Instead of using the Droid's native Phone app (see Chapter 5) to make telephone calls, you can make them with Google Voice instead. Google Voice (**Figure 9.6**) allows you to make telephone calls through Google and bypass the telecom carriers entirely.

This amazing service gives you a free telephone number that rings all your phones when someone calls it. It also allows you to make calls and send free text messages from this number. The best part is that when someone leaves a voicemail message in your Google Voice inbox, it's transcribed automatically and can be sent to you as an email or as an SMS text message. Conference calling and low-priced international calling round out an irresistible feature set.

Figure 9.6

The Google Voice inbox combines text and voice messages.

Google Listen

Price: Free
Developer: Google (http://listen.googlelabs.com)

Google Listen (**Figure 9.7**) displays your podcasts in a clean, well-organized screen where you can manage your podcast subscriptions and . . . well, *listen* to them. It's a simple concept that other apps tend to make needlessly complicated. Use Listen to search for podcasts, subscribe to the ones you like, and stream those podcasts directly to your Droid from just about anywhere. If you like podcasts, this app's well worth a try.

Figure 9.7
Google Listen is the best podcast app for Android because of its simplicity.

ShopSavvy

Price: Free
Developer: ShopSavvy, Inc. (http://shopsavvy.mobi)

ShopSavvy (**Figure 9.8**) turns your Droid into a portable comparison-shopping research assistant. It uses the phone's camera to scan the bar code on any product and then finds the best prices on the Internet and at nearby local stores. Just fire it up, point your Droid's camera at virtually any bar code, and wait for the beep. ShopSavvy displays a list of results for that item, including prices.

 Shop Savvy recently added support for scanning those funky square QR codes, too.

Figure 9.8
ShopSavvy compares prices over the Internet for anything with a bar code.

WeatherBug Elite

Price: $1.99
Developer: WeatherBug (http://weather.weatherbug.com/mobile.html)

Although several free weather apps are available for the Droid, WeatherBug is my favorite. It lets you view current conditions, forecasts, National Weather Service alerts, radar, maps, camera views, and video. It also offers location-based preferences and an excellent widget for your Droid's home screen.

The Elite version (**Figure 9.9**) includes enhanced contour weather maps showing lightning strikes, humidity, barometric pressure, and wind speed; radar animation; and an additional home-screen widget that displays an extended three-day forecast. My favorite feature is the locations summary screen, which displays weather conditions for all your saved locations.

Figure 9.9
WeatherBug Elite is the best weather app for the Droid—well worth the $2.

My Tracks for Android

Price: Free
Developer: Google (http://mytracks.appspot.com)

I bet that My Tracks (**Figure 9.10**) was developed by a team at Google that's into outdoor sports, because this app allows your Droid to record live GPS and output statistics about your run, hike, or bike ride over a given period, including your location, speed, distance, and elevation. You can upload all this data to Google Spreadsheets and Google Maps, and if you're competitive, you can even share your results with a friend. After you've captured several sets of data from your daily run or bike ride, you can track your progress.

To use My Tracks, make sure that GPS is turned on (touch Settings > Location & Security > Use GPS Satellites), launch the app, and touch Menu > Record Track. You'll see yourself represented as a small triangle on a Google map. Go do your thing, and when you're finished, touch Stop.

Whether you're a casual outdoors type or a diehard triathlete, you'll definitely get a kick out of My Tracks.

Figure 9.10

My Tracks can use your GPS coordinates to record your workout.

Twitter

Price: Free
Developer: Twitter (www.twitter.com)

I realize that Twitter is a love-it-or-hate-it type of thing, but if you love it, grab the officially sanctioned app from the mothership (**Figure 9.11**). Ever since Twitter released its own Android app, it's been the standard Twitter client on my Droid.

The free app offers real-time search, trending topics, and maps. It allows you to tweet; send direct messages; and share photos, videos, and links with your friends and the rest of the world.

Figure 9.11
The official Twitter app is my favorite in Android.

Locale

Price: $9.99
Developer: two forty four a.m. (www.twofortyfouram.com)

Locale (**Figure 9.12**) turns location management into an art form. This app manages all your Droid's settings dynamically, based on conditions such as location and time. You can use it to set up a condition that turns off 3G and switches to your home Wi-Fi network as soon as the phone is in range, for example. You can even set it up so that designated VIP callers always ring through, no matter how you've set the phone's ringer volume.

Figure 9.12

Locale allows you to set rules for things such as when and how your Droid rings.

Video Player

Price: Free
Developer: Jeff Hamilton, Google (www.google.com)

Although the Droid's Gallery app (which I cover in Chapter 8) scans the entire microSD card for media and will play video files, it's not a full-fledged video player. Luckily, third-party developers are addressing that omission.

For playing videos, I recommend Jeff Hamilton's basic Video Player (**Figure 9.13**). It plays video files from the SD card and supports numerous formats, including MPEG-4 or 3GPP with H.264 or H.263, as well as MP3, AAC, and AMR audio. Videos need to be 480 x 352 pixels or smaller to play back properly.

> **tip** If this app doesn't have enough horsepower for you, several other video-player apps are available in the Market, including VPlayer, Act 1, and mVideoPlayer.

Figure 9.13
Video Player is a basic video player for the Droid.

Titanium Backup Pro

Price: $5.99
Developer: RerWare (http://matrixrewriter.com/android)

Titanium Backup Pro (**Figure 9.14**) may not be the sexiest app in the Android Market, but if your Droid gets data-corrupted, lost, or damaged, you'll wish that you used it. It can restore data and apps easily on the same phone or a new one from your SD card or from the cloud (via Dropbox).

This app is the only one that can back up, restore, and freeze your apps, data, and Market links, including protected apps. After you set it up on a schedule with Dropbox, it does everything automatically, and you never have to worry about backing up again. Let's face it—nobody *always* remembers to back up.

Figure 9.14
Titanium Backup Pro can back up your Droid to Dropbox automatically.

ASTRO File Manager

Price: Free

Developer: Metago (www.metago.net/astro/fm)

ASTRO File Manager (**Figure 9.15**) gives you tools to manage all the files on your Droid. It won't be of much use to a novice user, but it's a tinkerer's dream come true. With this app, you can copy, move, delete, and rename files on your SD card. You can even work with multiple files and directories at the same time. The app runs in the background, so your actions will be completed even if you receive a phone call during the process.

ASTRO allows you to send files as attachments; view thumbnails and images; and even browse and create compressed files, including .zip and .tar. You can also use it to back up apps and manage running apps. It's literally a Swiss-army-knife app for Android.

Figure 9.15
ASTRO is the best file manager for Android, hands down.

Advanced Task Killer

Price: Free
Developer: ReChild (http://rechild.mobi)

Background apps are among the defining features of the Android operating system. It's handy to listen to a streaming Internet radio station while you're replying to email, for example. The problem is that apps running in the background consume precious battery life and other system resources. If you don't need to have them running, you'd be better off killing them.

Advanced Task Killer (**Figure 9.16**) is a super-handy app that lets you view, edit, and end any of the apps (processes) that are running on your Droid. You can also view the memory footprint of each app and instantly switch to any running app. On your schedule, Advanced Task Killer also frees all your memory except for the apps you specify, and it comes with a widget, too.

Figure 9.16
Advanced Task Killer stops unnecessary processes, saving battery life.

Amazon App for Android

Price: Free

Developer: Amazon (www.amazon.com/gp/anywhere/sms/android)

Amazon.com is America's largest online retailer and purveyor of everything from books and music to gourmet foods to electronics. Amazon makes it easy to buy with its combination of convenience, selection, and user-contributed reviews.

The Amazon App for Android (**Figure 9.17**) allows you to shop from your phone just as easily as you can from your computer. You can access your account, cart, wish lists, and all your various payment and shipment settings. The best feature, Amazon Remembers, allows you to search by bar code or photo. Simply snap a photo of a product with the Droid's camera, and Amazon responds with price comparisons and local purchasing options.

Figure 9.17
This app is a must-have if you shop Amazon. com often.

Google Goggles

Price: Free
Developer: Google (www.google.com/mobile/goggles)

Google Goggles lets you search the Web with your Droid's camera. If you don't want to type or speak your search query, you can search a third way: by photo.

With Goggles, you can take photos of bar codes and products like books and DVDs (just like you can with Amazon's app), but this app isn't limited to one store. Also, you can take photos of things like business cards, signs, artwork, and landmarks and then submit them for searching. Submitting a photo of a painting, for example, returns volumes of background information about it (**Figure 9.18**). Oh, and Goggles can solve sudoku puzzles, too.

Figure 9.18
Goggles allows you to search with your Droid's camera.

Google Sky Map

Price: Free

Developer: Google (www.google.com/sky/skymap.html)

Google Sky Map (**Figure 9.19**) is one of my favorite Android apps because it's fun and educational at the same time. Google Sky Map uses augmented reality (AR), which displays information from the Web in an overlay on your camera's live video feed. The technology is in its infancy, but it's already breathtaking and has a ton of potential.

With Google Sky Map, you just point your Droid at the night sky and browse planets, stars, and constellations on the screen of your phone. As you pan across the sky, the screen updates in real time, allowing you to match stars with their names. The app is very well done and well worth the download.

Figure 9.19
Google Sky Map turns your Droid into an annotated pocket telescope.

Pandora for Android

Price: Free

Developer: Pandora (www.pandora.com/android)

Pandora is my favorite music service, bar none. Its Droid app (**Figure 9.20**) allows you to stream music directly to your phone simply by entering an artist's name or a few keywords. The service searches the Music Genome Project—a huge catalog of music categorized by more than 400 musical attributes.

It's simple to set up a station based on an artist you like. I can't live without my Dub Reggae, Deep House, and Lounge radio stations, for example. Try setting up a station for Frank Sinatra for dinner music and even one for modern jazz, if that floats your boat.

Figure 9.20

Pandora streams free music directly to your Droid.

Facebook for Android

Price: Free
Developer: Facebook (www.facebook.com/android)

Whether you're a hard-core daily Facebook user or a casual one who checks in only periodically, you have lots of reasons to have this app installed on your Droid.

Facebook for Android (**Figure 9.21**) makes it easy to stay connected with your online friends. It allows you to share status updates, read your news feeds, and peruse your friends' walls and user information. You can also share photos easily and look up your friends' phone numbers right from the home screen.

Figure 9.21
Facebook for Android is essential for regular users of the social-networking site.

FlightTrack

Price: $4.99

Developer: Mobiata LLC (www.mobiata.com/apps/flighttrack-android)

FlightTrack (**Figure 9.22**) is the best app in its class because it has a super-clean interface and provides real-time flight itinerary updates at a glance. Its combination of usability and features is unmatched in the Android Market.

The app gives you all the tracking features you'd expect, including up-to-date data on flight cancellations, delays, and gate changes. Tapping any segment displays your full TripIt itinerary in the browser. FlightTrack will even alert you to flight status updates via push notifications even when the app isn't open.

Finally, when you're traveling, the cool home-screen widget is worth its weight in gold.

Figure 9.22

FlightTrack Pro is the best flight-tracking app for Android.

TouchDown

Price: $19.99
Developer: NitroDesk, Inc. (www.nitrodesk.com/TouchDown.aspx)

No, it's not a football game. TouchDown (**Figure 9.23**) is the preeminent Microsoft Exchange client for Android phones. If you need to use Exchange because your company uses it, just plunk down the $20, and look no further. TouchDown provides the most Exchange features and options of any app, including email, calendar, contacts, tasks, out-of-office reply, speech, and rules.

Figure 9.23

If you need to use Microsoft Exchange for work, TouchDown is a necessity.

The Honor Roll

You can use GPS technology in many fun and creative ways, thanks to some great third-party apps. Here are a few of my favorite location-aware apps in the Android Market:

- **Car Finder AR** ($3) uses AR, maps, and radar to help you find your parked car.

- **GasBot** ($7 per year) finds the cheapest gas near your current location.

- **Speed Proof** (free) lets you use your phone as a speedometer. Some people have beaten speeding tickets with GPS loggers.

- **TeeDroid Caddy** (free) measures the distance to the pin from your current location on the golf course.

- **Traffic Cams** (free) displays traffic and safety cameras near your location. Search for a free one for your area.

- **Wikitude World Browser** (free) is a reality browser that uses an Android phone's camera and compass to layer AR information over the live camera image.

10

Resources

I hope that this *Pocket Guide* helped you get up and running on your Droid quickly. If you'd like to do further research on any of the topics that I covered, the Internet has a wealth of additional information that you can peruse on your own schedule.

In this chapter, I list several useful Web sites that can further your knowledge of all things Droid.

Phone Links

Because Google is so tightly integrated with the Droid, you'll find your-self using a lot of its products online in a desktop Web browser. Here are a few Web sites that you'll want to use to get the most out of your Droid:

Droid Bionic (Motorola)
www.motorola.com/mydroidbionic

Droid Pro (Motorola)
www.motorola.com/mydroidpro

Droid 2 (Motorola)
www.motorola.com/mydroid2

Droid X (Motorola)
www.motorola.com/mydroidx

Droid Incredible (HTC)
www.htc.com/us/products/droid-incredible-verizon

Droid Eris (HTC)
www.htc.com/us/products/droid-eris-verizon

Droid 1 (Motorola)
www.motorola.com/mydroid

Droid Does
www.droiddoes.com

note Unlike the printed pages you're reading, the Internet changes rapidly, and so can these links. Keep an eye out for new and different URLs as new models come out.

Google Links

Because Google is so tightly integrated with the Droid, you'll find yourself using many of its products online in a desktop Web browser. Here are a few Web sites that you'll want to use to get the most out of your Droid:

Gmail
www.google.com/mail

Google Calendar
www.google.com/calendar

Google Contacts
www.google.com/contacts

Google Latitude
www.google.com/latitude

Google Maps
www.google.com/maps

Google Voice
www.google.com/voice

YouTube
www.youtube.com

Mobile apps

To find out more about Google's mobile apps, like the ones that ship on the Droid, just add the word *mobile* to the URL, as follows:

Gmail for Mobile
www.google.com/mobile/mail

Google Goggles
www.google.com/mobile/goggles

Google Maps for Mobile
www.google.com/mobile/maps

Google Maps Navigation
www.google.com/mobile/navigation

Google Voice for Mobile
www.google.com/mobile/voice

YouTube for Mobile
www.google.com/mobile/youtube

note **Many Google mobile sites have excellent instructional videos showing the apps in action.**

Google blogs

Google blogs are probably the best sources of information about the company's products. Extremely talented Google engineers and product managers wax poetic in their blogs about the company's latest products, and information breaks there first. Here are a few good blogs to follow:

Google Lat Long Blog
http://google-latlong.blogspot.com

Official Google Blog
http://googleblog.blogspot.com

Official Google Mobile Blog
http://googlemobile.blogspot.com

tip If you really have a lot of time on your hands, Google lists almost 100 blogs in its blog directory, organized by products, ads, developers, region, and Googlewide. You'll find the directory at www.google.com/press/blogs/directory.html.

Android Developer Challenge (ADC)

Each year, Google holds the Android Developer Challenge (ADC), giving prizes for the best applications for the Android operating system. The company awards a $100,000 top prize, $50,000 second prize, and $25,000 third prize in each of ten categories, including Lifestyle, Productivity, and Games. The stakes are high, and winning apps get a big spike in sales after the winners are announced.

Find out about the ADC here:

http://code.google.com/android/adc/gallery_winners.html

YouTube

Because Google owns YouTube, it's logical that the ubiquitous video player would end up on the Droid. In the very definition of a symbiotic relationship, Google also posts all its Android tutorial videos on YouTube, and they're fantastic resources. Check out these sites:

Google: Google's Channel
www.youtube.com/user/Google

Official Android Tips: AndroidTips's Channel
www.youtube.com/androidtips

Support links

If the phone links earlier in this chapter don't answer your questions, try some of these support links, which provide lots of information and technical support:

Droid by Motorola Tech Specs
www.motorola.com/Consumers/US-EN/Consumer-Product-and-Services/Mobile-Phones/ci.Motorola-DROID-US-EN.alt

Motorola Owners' Forum
https://supportforums.motorola.com

Software Update: Droid Eris by HTC
http://support.vzw.com/information/droid_eris_upgrade.html

System Update: Droid by Motorola
http://support.vzw.com/information/droid_upgrade.html

Third-Party Links

In addition to all the Web sites maintained by Google and its manufacturing and carrier partners, you can find hundreds that are painstakingly
updated by members of the Android community, including these:

AndGeeks
www.andgeeks.com

Android Central
www.androidcentral.com

AndroidGuys
www.androidguys.com

Android Tapp
www.androidtapp.com

Hello Android
www.helloandroid.com

IntoMobile: Android
www.intomobile.com/category/platforms/android

TmoNews: Android
www.tmonews.com/category/android

@Twitter

Many Android bloggers and developers maintain Twitter accounts. Here are some of the accounts whose tweets you need to follow:

Android Central
http://twitter.com/androidcentral

AndroidGuys.com
http://twitter.com/androidguys

Droid Buzz
http://twitter.com/droidbuzz

HTC
http://twitter.com/htc

Verizon Wireless
http://twitter.com/verizonwireless

That's a Wrap

So there you have it, folks! You've had a good look at everything from unboxing your Droid to configuring it to installing applications on it.

I hope that you enjoyed reading this book as much as I enjoyed writing it. More important, I hope that it helps you squeeze every little bit of potential out of your Droid.

Index